AF818928

JANUA LINGUARUM

STUDIA MEMORIAE
NICOLAI VAN WIJK DEDICATA

edenda curat

C. H. VAN SCHOONEVELD

Indiana University

Series Minor, 128

ON MACHINE TRANSLATION

Selected Papers

by

PAUL L. GARVIN

1972
MOUTON
THE HAGUE · PARIS

© Copyright 1972 in The Netherlands.
Mouton & Co. N.V., Publishers, The Hague.

No part of this book may be translated or reproduced in any form, by print, photoprint, microfilm, or any other means, without written permission from the publishers.

LIBRARY OF CONGRESS CATALOG CARD NUMBER: 79-182469

Printed in Belgium by NICI, Printers, Ghent

ACKNOWLEDGEMENTS

Permission to reprint these articles from the following sources is gratefully acknowledged:

A linguist's view of language-data processing, *Natural Language and the Computer*, ed. by Paul L. Garvin (New York, McGraw-Hill, 1963).

Some comments on algorithm and grammar in the automatic parsing of natural languages, *Mechanical Translation*, vol. 9, 1, 1966.

The Georgetown-IBM experiment of 1954: An evaluation in retrospect, *Papers in Linguistics in Honor of Léon Dostert* (The Hague, Mouton, 1967), 46-56.

Some linguistic problems in machine translation, *For Roman Jakobson* (The Hague, Mouton, 1956), 180-186.

Machine translation, *Proceedings of the VIII International Congress of Linguists* (Oslo, Oslo University Press, 1958), 502-508.

Syntactic retrieval: A first approximation to operational machine translation, *Proceedings of the National Symposium on Machine Translation. Held at the University of California, Los Angeles, February 2-5, 1960*, ed. by H. P. Edmundson (Englewood Cliffs, N. J., Prentice-Hall, 1961), 286-292.

Machine translation today: The fulcrum approach and heuristics, *Lingua* 21 (Amsterdam, North Holland Publishing Co., 1968), 162-182.

Degrees of computer participation in linguistic research, *Language*, vol. 38, 4 (Baltimore, Linguistic Society of America, 1962), 385-389.

The impact of language data processing on linguistic analysis, *Proceedings of the Ninth International Congress of Linguists, Cambridge, Mass.*, 1962 (The Hague, Mouton, 1964), 706-712.

CONTENTS

INTRODUCTION*

In the early and middle fifties, a number of news stories appeared here and there announcing "fundamental breakthroughs" in the development of machine translation from Russian into English and declaring that workable machine translation systems, if not already a reality, were just around the corner. Since then, one or two government agencies in the United States have begun to operate automatic translation facilities with which some users were partly satisfied, some not at all, and none completely. More recently, a committee constituted by the National Academy of Sciences (of the United States), National Research Council — the Automatic Language Processing Advisory Committee (ALPAC) — conducted a two-year study of the field of machine translation and came to the conclusion that "without recourse to human translation or editing ... none is in immediate prospect".[1]

Where, then, do we stand in machine translation? Were the claims justified that were made in the earlier days, or is ALPAC correct in concluding that there is no prospect for its achievement in the foreseeable future?

In my opinion, both are wrong.

To substantiate my view, let me give a brief survey of the state of machine translation. First, let me make clear that the field of machine translation is (with one glaring exception — the photo-

* The opinions expressed here were originally voiced in P. L. Garvin, "Machine Translation — Fact or Fancy?" *Datamation,* April 1967, pp. 29-31.

1 *Language and Machines, Computers in Translation and Linguistics.* A Report by the Automatic Language Processing Advisory Committee, National Academy of Sciences, National Research Council. Publication 1416. National Academy of Sciences, National Research Council. Washington, D.C., 1966. p. 19.

scopic disc)[2] not primarily concerned with the design of a special translation machine, but with the design of translation programs to be run on large general-purpose computers. Let me add that the major effort so far in this country has been directed toward the machine translation of Russian into English, although some experimental work has also been done on other languages (such as Chinese and German).

Two extreme approaches have been taken to the field, and one which I consider a reasonable middle ground. I call the two extremes the "brute-force" approach and the "perfectionist" approach. Let me discuss these first, since they are the ones represented in the earlier newspaper claims and in the recent ALPAC opinion.

The "brute-force" approach is based on the assumption that, given a sufficiently large memory, machine translation can be accomplished without a complex algorithm — either with a very large dictionary containing not only words but also phrases, or with a large dictionary and an equally large table of grammar rules taken from conventional Russian grammar. The dictionary approach was implemented on special hardware, the dictionary-plus-conventional-grammar approach on a general-purpose computer. Both versions of the "brute-force" approach have yielded translations on a fairly large scale, but of questionable quality. The trouble is that both systems are fundamentally unimprovable, since they allow only mechanical extensions of the tables which create as many or more new errors as they rectify. The negative opinion of ALPAC regarding the achievements of machine translation is based largely on a study of these systems, and is of course justified to the extent to which it concerns them.

The "perfectionist" approach represents the other extreme. It is based on the assumption that without a complete theoretical knowledge of the source and target languages (based on a theoretical knowledge of language in general), as well as a perfect understanding of the process of translation, both preferably in the form of mathematical models, the task can not even be begun. Conse-

2 Neil Macdonald, "The Photoscopic Language Translator", *Computers and Automation*, Aug. 1960, pp. 6-8.

quently, the "perfectionists" have devoted most of their energies to theoretical studies of language, sometimes using computing equipment in the process, and have deferred the development of actual translation systems into the indefinite future. ALPAC's assessment of the future of the field reflects this view.

Clearly, neither extreme will lead to acceptable machine translation within the foreseeable future (or perhaps ever). But there is that reasonable middle ground — to which, in my opinion, ALPAC has not given sufficient attention. Not surprisingly, it is the position that I represent.

The approach which I have been taking is essentially an engineering solution to the problem. It avoids not only the naïveté of the "brute-force" approach (which by now has become evident to the professional world thanks to the poor quality of the results that it has produced), but it also avoids the lack of task-orientation of the "perfectionist" approach (which is much less evident to a professional world that stands in awe of theoretical research couched in dazzling quasi-mathematical symbolisms).

My disagreements with the "perfectionists" deserve some further elaboration.

It is clear that the achievement of acceptable machine translation requires a very detailed and extensive knowledge of the languages concerned. Everybody agrees on this. Where the disagreement lies is in regard to the nature of this knowledge and the approach to be used in acquiring it. In my opinion, the knowledge needed for the design of machine-translation systems is not merely theoretical knowledge, but primarily empirical knowledge, and above all problem-solving engineering know-how. This knowledge cannot be acquired in the abstract, before the design of translation systems is begun. On the contrary, it is only in the process of developing a translation algorithm that it becomes clear what type of knowledge of the language is required. And it is only in the process of experimenting with the algorithm that the correctness of our findings about language can be verified.

Most of this discussion is now largely "academic", since the generous support which has characterized the earlier days of machine translation has been reduced to a trickle, and it is obvious that the transition from a well-conceived and elaborated plan to an operational system is an extremely expensive proposition.

The papers assembled in this volume show the extent to which an engineering approach to machine translation is feasible and how close to operational realization it has been developed.

Buffalo, New York, June 1970 PAUL L. GARVIN

I

CONTEXT

A LINGUIST'S VIEW OF LANGUAGE-DATA PROCESSING

Language-data processing is a relatively new field of endeavor. As with all new fields, the exact area it covers is not completely defined. Even the term *language-data processing* is not yet generally accepted, although its use is increasing.

The definition of the field of language-data processing given here includes the application of any data-processing equipment to natural-language text — that is, not only the application of computing machinery, but also the application of the less powerful punched-card and tabulating equipment. It may even be reasonable to say that a purely intellectual procedure for the treatment of language data, which by its rigor and logic attempts to simulate, or allow for, the application of data-processing equipment, is a form of language-data processing, or at least a data-processing approach to language analysis.

From a linguist's standpoint two purposes can be served by language-data processing:

The first of these is linguistic analysis, which will ultimately and ideally include the use of data-processing equipment to obtain analytic linguistic results.

The second purpose is the use of language-data processing in information handling, where linguistics is auxiliary to the major objective. Here language-data processing is of interest for applied linguistics. It is also of interest as an area in which the usefulness and perhaps even the validity of analytic linguistic results can be tested.

Concretely, language-data processing for linguistic analysis will primarily include *automatic linguistic analysis* or at least automatic aids or automatic preliminaries to linguistic analysis. Language-data processing for information handling includes such fields as machine translation, information storage and retrieval (if based on natural language), automatic abstracting, certain other data-processing applications, and the like. All these activities can be summed up under the heading of *linguistic information processing.* The two aspects of language-data processing are related in that the results of the former can be utilized in the latter. Sometimes this is not only desirable but necessary.

The area of linguistic information processing can be divided into two major subareas: (1) machine translation; and (2) information retrieval, automatic abstracting, and related activities, all of which may be summarized under the heading of *content processing.* There are two criteria for this division. One is the degree to which the results of linguistic analysis are considered necessary for the purpose. In machine translation none of the serious workers in the field will deny the usefulness of linguistic analysis or linguistic information; on the other hand, a number of approaches to information retrieval and automatic abstracting are based on statistical considerations, and linguistics is considered a useful but not essential ingredient.

Another criterion by which to distinguish between the two subareas of this field is more interesting from the linguist's standpoint. This is the manner in which the content of the document is to be utilized. In machine translation the major objective is to recognize the content of a document in order to render it in another language. In content processing the recognition is only the first step. The principal objective here is to evaluate the content in order to process it further for a given purpose. This evaluation requires the automatic inclusion of some kind of relevance criterion by means of which certain portions of the document can be highlighted and other portions can be ignored. The criterion for such an evaluation in the case of information retrieval seems to be the comparability of each particular document to those of a related set; common features and differences can serve as a basis for an index in terms of which information can be retrieved in response to a request. In automatic abstracting, various portions of the document are compared and on the basis of their relative significance are retained or omitted from the condensed version.

It is apparent that the evaluation of content poses a somewhat more complex problem for the investigator than its mere recognition. It is not surprising, therefore, that the linguistic contributions to content processing have so far been much less conclusive than the contributions that linguists have made to machine translation. It is on the other hand equally apparent, at least to the linguist, that a linguistic approach has an important contribution to make to content processing, especially if a product of high quality is desired.

It is also worth noting in this connection that important negative opinions have been voiced with regard to both aspects of language-data processing. N. Chomsky takes the strong position that a discovery procedure — that is, a fixed set of rules for the discovery of relevant elements — is not a realistic goal for a science such as linguistics. This implies, of course, that automatic linguistic analysis also is an unreasonable proposition. Y. Bar-Hillel, a well-known symbolic logician and a philosophical critic of language-data processing, takes an equally clear-cut position. In a survey of machine translation in the United States conducted on behalf of the Office of Naval Research, he made the well-known statement that fully automatic, high-quality machine translation is impossible.[1] He has voiced a similarly negative view in regard to other aspects of practical language-data processing.[2]

Needless to say, in spite of the need for objective criticism and an awareness of the difficulties involved, a more positive attitude toward the field is a prerequisite for active participation in the research.

The present discussion concerns the problems of language-data processing in both senses as related to the assumed properties of natural language. We shall follow the problem through the system

[1] Y. Bar-Hillel, "The Present Status of Automatic Translation of Languages", in F. L. Alt (ed.), *Advances in Computers*, New York, London, 1960, pp. 91-163.

[2] Y. Bar-Hillel, "Some Theoretical Aspects of the Mechanization of Literature Searching", in Walter Hoffman (ed.), *Digital Information Processors*, Interscience Publishers, New York, 1962, pp. 406-443.

by going from input to internal phase. We shall not consider the mechanics of the output, since at present linguistics has little or no contribution to make to this question.

AUTOMATIC SPEECH RECOGNITION AND CHARACTER RECOGNITION

All present-day language-data-processing activities use the conventional input mechanisms of punched card, punched-paper tape, magnetic tape, or the like. This is generally considered to be a major bottleneck in terms of practicality since the cost, especially for the large quantities of input that are desirable for eventual production, is prohibitive. A good deal of effort in various places is therefore directed toward automating the input.

To accommodate the two usual manifestations of the sign components of languages — the phonetic and the graphic — efforts toward automating input proceed in two directions: *automatic speech recognition* and *automatic character recognition.* The purpose is to design a perceptual device which will be capable of identifying either spoken or written signals for transposition into the machine code required by a computer. Needless to say, this objective is of considerable interest to the linguist, and linguistics has a significant potential contribution to make, especially in the case of speech recognition.

The problem in speech recognition is one of identifying, within the total acoustic output of the human voice or its mechanical reproduction, those elements which are significant for communication. The difficulty of the problem becomes apparent when one realizes that most phoneticians agree that only a small portion of the total energy in the human voice output (some claim as little as 1 per cent) is utilized for purposes of the linguistic signal proper. The remaining energy serves as a signal for such nonlinguistic elements as the identification of the sex and individuality of the speaker, his state of health (whether or not he has a cold), his emotional state, and a large number of other behavioral indices. Thus, the acoustic power available for purposes of speech recognition appears to be rather small. The significant fact here is that this small percentage tends to be masked by the rest. The second difficulty is that the natural vocal signal is semicontinuous; that is, the number of physically observable breaks in the continuity of the stream of human speech is much smaller than the number of discrete elements into which the signal may be decomposed in either alphabetic writing or linguistic analysis.

The problem in phonemic analysis is one of transposing a semicontinuous natural signal into a series of discrete elements. To give an example, a short utterance such as *time* is revealed by acoustic instruments to consist of essentially two distinct physical portions: a burst following a pause representing the element /*t*/, and a set of harmonic elements extending over a given period and with no observable major interruptions. In terms of phonemic analysis, on the other hand, the utterance *time* is usually interpreted to consist of four discrete units: the phonemes /*t*/, /*a*/, /*y*/, and /*m*/. The method by which the phonemic analyst arrives at this decomposition of the continuous span into its presumed underlying components is one of comparison, based on his assumptions about the dimensional structure of language. The /*t*/ is isolated by comparing *time* to *dime*; the /*a*/ is isolated by comparing *time* with *team*; the /*y*/ is isolated by comparing *time* to *town*; and the /*m*/ is isolated by comparing *time* to *tide*. The analyst gains his initial knowledge of the speech signal from his interpretation of what he hears. Not until an initial description of the elementary discrete units has been obtained does the analyst proceed to investigate the structure of phonemic fused units of a higher order of complexity such as syllables or the phonemic analogs of orthographic words.

It is not unreasonable to suppose, on the other hand, that an ideal speech-recognition device may deal directly with the semicontinuous *phonetic stretches* that are observable in the stream of speech, and that may turn out to correspond, roughly or precisely, to the fused units of phonemic analysis. The perceptual mechanism which would constitute the first component of such a device would then have to meet two objectives: first, to recognize pertinent points of interruption in the stream of speech in order to find the boundaries of the phonetic stretches; and second, to recognize, within the total energy spectrum of the human vocal signal, those particular acoustic features of each stretch that are relevant to the transmission of the spoken message.

The present state of speech recognition resembles the early stages of phonemic analysis in the sense that experiments so far have been largely limited to machine perception of short isolated stretches comparable to the short isolated examples elicited by an analyst in the beginning of his work. Just as in phonemics these short examples are used to determine an initial inventory of vowels and consonants, so the present speech-recognition work on short stretches is directed toward an identification of vocalic and consonantal features. Even in this limited framework, progress has so far resulted in the identification of only some of the gross acoustic features, such as the break between syllables, the friction component of certain consonants, and the voicing component of vowels and certain consonants. More refined identifications can be expected as acoustic research progresses, and an adequate capability for identifying isolated phonetic stretches is quite conceivable.[3]

Little attention has been given so far to machine recognition of the interruptions in the continuity of the stream of speech that linguists call *junctures*. Linguistic and acoustic research on the phonetic characteristics of junctures will undoubtedly make significant contributions to this aspect of speech recognition.

Assuming that a perception mechanism can acquire the capability of recognizing both the boundaries and the characteristic features of the phonetic stretches of normal speech, there still remains a significant phase of speech recognition which goes beyond the perceptual. From the stretches that have been recognized, the complete device must in some way compute a linguistically relevant input for the internal phase of the data-processing system; that is, the speech-recognition device, after having identified

[3] Claims to that effect have been made since this paper was originally written.

phonetic stretches on the basis of their perceptual characteristics, must transform them into strings of linguistic signs — morphemes. For practical purposes the device might have to transform sound types not into morphemes, but into printed words or their binary representations.

Consider the problem in terms of an immediate application of speech recognition: the *voicewriter*. This device is intended to transmit the spoken message to a typewriter to obtain as output a typewritten version of the message.

It is clear that a good many of the pecularities of a typewritten document, even not counting problems presented by orthography in the narrower sense, are not directly contained as vocal signals in the spoken message. These details would include paragraphing, capitalization, and punctuation. In dictation such features of the document are either left to the secretary or indicated by editorial comments. Thus, even assuming a functioning perception mechanism, some provision would have to be made for details of this type — for instance, a capacity for receiving and executing verbal orders similar to the editorial comments for the secretary.

The problems posed by the orthography in the narrower sense — that is, the actual spelling conventions for particular words — vary to the extent that the writing system deviates from the spoken form of the language. It becomes a translation problem, comparable to the problem of translating by machine from one language to another. The same spoken form may well correspond to more than one written form, and this ambiguity then has to be resolved by context searching, which is a syntactic operation analogous to its equivalent in machine translation. Thus, assuming that the perception mechanism has identified a phonetic stretch */riyd/*, the voicewriter may have to represent it in typescript as either *reed* or *read,* depending on whether it occurred in a sentence dealing with *a reed in the wind* or a sentence dealing with *reading.*

An additional context-searching routine, comparable to the "missing-word routines" used in machine translation for dealing with words that are not found in the machine dictionary, will probably have to be included for the identification of "poor" phonetic stretches — that is, those that do not have enough signal strength or are not pronounced clearly enough to be recognizable by the perception mechanism.

At the present state of the art is appears that it may not be necessary to go through a three-step computation sequence from phonetic stretches to phonemes to morphemes or written words, but that a direct computation of morphemes or written words from phonetic stretches can be envisioned. This computation would be carried out by means of a dictionary of phonetic stretches stored in memory, to be processed by appropriate ambiguity-resolution and missing-form routines. (This conception of the linguistic aspects of the speech-recognition problem stems from Madeleine Mathiot, personal communication.)[4]

The problem of character recognition is by comparison somewhat less complex, because — unless one thinks of a device for recognizing handwriting — the visual input into the device is discrete — that is, it can be expected to consist of separately printed or typed letters or characters. Thus, the very difficult speech-recognition problem of recognizing the boundaries of stretches within a semicontinuous signal does not exist for character recognition. On the other hand, the problem of recognizing what particular features of the signal — in terms of strokes, angles, curves, directions, and the like — are relevant to the function of the character is similar to the problem of recognizing the linguistically relevant acoustic features of speech. A further advantage of character recognition is that no computation is required to give orthographic representation to the visual signal, since the signal is orthographic to begin with. Linguists have generally given much less thought to the structure of writing systems in terms of their differentiating characteristics than they have to the phonological structure of speech and its relevant distinctive features. Thus, the linguistic contribution to the field of character recognition has been quite trivial so far. It seems that the recognition of relevant

[4] For a detailed discussion of this problem, see now Paul L. Garvin and Edith C. Trager, "The Conversion of Phonetic into Orthographic English: A Machine-Translation Approach to the Problem", *Phonetica* 11. 1-18 (1964).

properties of shape such as the ones enumerated above is closely related to the problem of recognizing visual shapes in general, and therefore is less closely related to linguistics than is the problem of speech recognition.

Where linguistics can make a contribution is in the recognition of poorly printed or otherwise unrecognizable characters, for the gaps in the recognition string will have to be filled by a context-searching routine similar in principle to that required for speech recognition.

One of the fundamental difficulties in the area of character recognition seems to be the variety of fonts that are used in ordinary print and typing. Devices which are limited to a single font — particularly if that font has been specifically designed to facilitate the operation of the device — are now in an operational stage. On the other hand, devices which can deal with a multiplicity of fonts, particularly fonts with which the device has had no prior "experience", are still in their infancy. Some experiments have already yielded data about those characteristics which different fonts have in common and on which a common recognition routine can be based. Work is in progress on the particular perceptive mechanisms which could optimally serve to recognize these characteristics. In this respect, the field of character recognition appears to be closer to practical results than the field of speech recognition.

AUTOMATIC LINGUISTIC ANALYSIS

From a linguist's standpoint, the internal phase of language-data processing involves two types of activities: automatic linguistic analysis on the one hand and linguistic information processing on the other.

An automatic linguistic-analysis program is here defined as a computer program which, given as input a body of text, will produce as output a linguistic description of the system of the natural language represented by the text. A corollary capability of such a program will be the capacity for deciding whether or not a given input indeed constitutes a text in a natural language.

We can conceive of the system of a language as an orderly aggregate of various kinds of elements, each of which has a finite and typical set of co-occurrence possibilities with regard to other elements of the system. The elements are of different functional types and orders of complexity, as exemplified by such elements of written English as letters, syllables, words, or phrases. These elements recur in texts in a regular way, so as to form *distribution* classes in terms of shared co-occurrence characteristics. Here the purpose of linguistic analysis is to specify the nature and boundaries of the various types and orders of elements, as well as to describe the co-occurrence patterns serving as the criteria for the definition of the distribution classes, and to list the membership of these classes. The former aspect of linguistic analysis is often termed *segmentation,* the latter is called *distributional analysis.*

Linguistic segmentation is the first step in the analysis of raw text — that is, spoken messages recorded from native informants. Segmentation procedures are based on the relation between the form (i.e., the phonetic shape) and the meaning (in operational terms, the translation or possible paraphrase) of the message. Their mechanization thus would require the comparative processing of two inputs — one representing the phonetic shape of the raw text and the other its translation or paraphrase.

A program designed for a single rather than a dual input hence cannot be expected to accomplish segmentation.[5] We can therefore suggest that the initial inventory of elementary units not be compiled automatically but that the automatic processing of the text for purposes of linguistic analysis use a previously segmented input consisting of units already delimited. This could be a text segmented into morphemic segments by a linguistic analyst or, the more practical alternative, a text in conventional spelling with orthographic word boundaries marked by spaces, and punctuation

[5] For an approach using a computer system interacting with a native informant for automatic segmentation, see now Paul L. Garvin, "The Automation of Discovery Procedure in Linguistics", *Language* 43.172-8 (1967). Reprinted in *On Linguistic Method. Selected Papers by Paul L. Garvin,* 2nd edition. The Hague, Mouton & Co., 1971, pp. 38-47.

indicating certain other boundaries. The type of linguistic analysis to be performed on this previously segmented input would then be one of classifying the elementary input units on the basis of their relevant cooccurrence properties. That is, automatic linguistic analysis would essentially be a distributional analysis by a computer program.

The intended output of such a distributional analysis program would be a dictionary listing of all the elements (for instance, all the printed words) found to recur in the input text, with each element in the listing accompanied by a grammar code reflecting the distributional description of the element in terms of the distribution class and subclass to which it belongs. Since the purpose of the program thus is to produce a grammar-coded dictionary listing, it is logically necessary to require that the program itself initially contain no dictionary or grammar code, but only the routines required for their compilation.

The basic question of distributional analysis is: does unit *a* occur in environment *b*? This question can be answered by a computer program. The problem is primarily one of specifying automatically what units *a* the question is to be asked about, and what environments *b* are to be considered in arriving at an answer.

In ordinary linguistic analysis, informant responses are evaluated and text is examined "manually" in order to arrive at distributional descriptions by using diagnostic contexts. The difficulty of informant work, as all linguists know, is the element of subjectivity inherent in the use of a human informant. This subjectivity is maximized by using one's own self as an informant; it may be minimized by circumscribing the test situation very narrowly and by using a variety of informants, as well as other controls. However, as the questions become more sophisticated, the informant's responses become more and more difficult to control and his memory becomes less and less reliable. Thus, even in ordinary linguistic analysis one reaches a point where informant work has to be combined with the study of text.

The basic difficulty in the use of text for purposes of linguistic analysis is that large samples are required. This is understandable if one takes into account the inverse ratio of the recurrence of elements to the size of sample: The less frequently an element recurs, the larger the sample required in order to study its distributional properties. Data-processing equipment allows the processing of very large bodies of text using the same program. At the present time, lack of speech- or character-recognition devices is the greatest practical bottleneck requiring considerable expense at the input end for keypunching or related purposes.

From the linguist's standpoint, these difficulties are balanced primarily by the advantage of the increased reliability of data-processing equipment and the possibility of attaining a rigor hitherto not customary in the field. Once costs can be brought down, there is the promise of an ultimate operational capability for processing much larger samples of language than the linguist can ever hope to examine manually. Finally, even without access to extensive programming and computer time, a partial implementation of automatic analysis can be expected to yield interesting results.

A fully automatic distributional analysis program can be looked upon as a heuristic rather than a purely algorithmic problem. A. L. Samuels has set forth some of the characteristics of an intellectual activity in which heuristic procedures and learning processes can play a major role. As applied to the problem of playing checkers, these are as follows:[6]

1. The activity must not be deterministic in the practical sense. There exists no known algorithm which will guarantee a win or draw in checkers, and the complete exploitation of every possible path through a checker game would involve perhaps 10^{40} choices of moves which, at 3 choices per millimicrosecond, would still take 10^{21} centuries to consider.

2. A definite goal must exist — the winning of the game — and at least one criterion of intermediate goal must exist which has

[6] A. L. Samuels, "Some Studies in Machine Learning Using the Game of Checkers", *IBM Journal of Research and Development*, pp. 211-212, July, 1959. Quoted by permission.

bearing on the achievement of the final goal and for which the sign should be known. ...

3. The rules of the activity should be definite and they should be known. ...

4. There should be a background of knowledge of the activity against which the learning progress can be tested.

5. The activity should be one that is familiar to a substantial body of people so that the behavior of the program can be made understandable to them. ...

The above criteria seem to be applicable to automatic linguistic analysis as well, paraphrased as follows:

1. Linguistic analysis is not deterministic in the practical sense. There exists no known algorithm which will guarantee success in linguistic analysis, and the complete exploitation of every possible combinatory criterion might involve an equally astronomical number of steps as the number of moves to be explored in a checkers algorithm.

2. A definite goal does exist — a detailed distributional statement — and criteria can be formulated for intermediate goals that have bearing on the achievement of the final goal. These would be the broader distributional statements from which the ultimate, more refined classifications can be derived. Unlike checkers, the final goal can not be formulated as simply.

3. The rules of the activity are definite and can be formulated. This, of course, presupposes that one accepts as a basic assumption the possibility of linguistic discovery procedures. The procedures that apply here are those of substitution and dropping; they can be made computable, and they may be introduced into the heuristic linguistic-analysis program after certain necessary preliminary steps have been completed. Other equally computable procedures can be formulated.

4. There is, of course, a background of knowledge of the activity against which the machine results are tested: Linguistic analysis is, or can be made into, an established field and machine results can be compared to human results.

5. Although the activity of linguistic analysis is not one that is familiar to a substantial body of people, its results nonetheless can be compared to the intuitive behavior of an entire speech community, and the behavior of the program can be explicated in terms of this observed intuitive behavior.

It is thus possible to envision a computer program which will process the initially segmented text by applying to it a variety of linguistic analytic procedures, and will evaluate the results of each trial on the basis of certain built-in statistical or otherwise computable criteria. The program, operating in an alternation of such trial and evaluation routines, can be expected to accept certain trials and reject others on the basis of these criteria. The results of the initial tests performed by the program can then be utilized for the automatic formulation of additional tests leading to a more refined classification, until the potential of the program is exhausted and the output can be printed out for inspection by a competent linguistic evaluator.

Such a program will be particularly interesting for the analysis of languages in which word classes — that is, parts of speech — are not easily definable and where conspicuous formal marks of syntactic relations are either absent or infrequent. Examples of such languages are Chinese and English.[7]

MACHINE TRANSLATION

Let us now turn from automatic linguistic analysis to linguistic information processing. The activities in the latter field can be divided into two major categories: machine translation on the one hand and content processing on the other.

Prior to machine translation, descriptive linguists were mostly

[7] For the detailed discussion of a proposed program of automatic linguistic analysis, see Paul L. Garvin, "Automatic Linguistic Analysis — a Heuristic Problem", *1961 International Conference on Machine Translation of Languages and Applied Language Analysis*, vol. 2, pp. 655-669, London, 1962. Reprinted in *On Linguistic Method, Selected Papers by Paul L. Garvin*, 2nd edition, The Hague, Mouton & Co., 1971, pp. 112-131.

concerned with the formal features of language and considered linguistic meaning only to the extent to which it has bearing on formal distinctions. In translation on the other hand — both human and machine translation — meaning becomes the primary subject of interest. Relations between forms are no longer dealt with for their own sake; they are now treated in terms of the function they have as carriers of meaning. Meaning is granted an independent theoretical existence of a sort, since it is only by assuming a content as separate from the form of a particular language that one can decide whether a passage in one language is indeed the translation of a passage in another language: they are if they both express the same, or at least roughly the same, content; they are not if they do not.

In the process of translation the expression of the content in one language is replaced by the expression of an equivalent content in another. To mechanize the process, the recognition of the content in its first expression, the *source language,* must be mechanized; then the command can be generated to give the same content another linguistic expression in the *target language.* A machine-translation program must therefore contain a *recognition routine* to accomplish the first objective, and a *command routine* to accomplish the second. Since the command routine presupposes the recognition routine and not conversely, a "recognition grammar" of this sort is more essential for purposes of machine translation than a "generative grammar".

For recognition of the content of the source document, the machine-translation program has to take into account, and can take advantage of, the structural properties of the language in which the content is originally expressed. In a sense, one structural property has already been accounted for by the nature of the input: the two levels of structuring, the graphemic and the morphemic, are utilized in the input by sensing the text letter by letter and recognizing spaces, punctuation marks, and special symbols. The graphemic input then has to be processed for morphemic recognition: the program has to ascertain what content-bearing element is represented by each combination of letters — that is, printed word between spaces — that has been sensed at the input. In order to effect this identification, the program can and must draw on the other two sets of levels of natural language: the two levels of organization, and the levels of integration.

The two levels of organization, those of selection and arrangement, are represented in the program by the *machine dictionary* and the *translation algorithm* respectively. It is obvious that in order to produce a non-ridiculous translation, a program must contain not only a dictionary but also an algorithm. The function of the algorithm is dual: it must select from several possible dictionary equivalents that which is applicable to the particular sentence to be translated; it also must achieve the rearrangement of the words of the translation, whenever this is necessary in order to give the appropriate expression to the content of the original. To make possible the generation of these selection and rearrangement commands, the algorithm must be capable of recognizing the syntactic and other conditions under which these commands are necessary and appropriate. For this recognition to be effective, the levels of integration of the language — that is, the fused units of varying orders of complexity — have to be taken into account. Fused units have to be identified as to their boundaries and functions. The details of this problem are discussed in later papers in this volume.

In an early theoretical paper on machine translation by this author[8] the statement was made that "The extent of machine translatability is limited by the amount of information contained within the same sentence". Since the sentence is the maximum domain of necessary linguistic relationships, a translation algorithm based on fixed linguistic rules appears to be limited to this domain. Later experience has shown that such *deterministic rules* are, however, not the only possible translation rules. In order to deal with relations across sentence boundaries, it is necessary to assume that in addition to deterministic rules, *probabilistic rules*

[8] Paul L. Garvin, "Some Linguistic Problems in Machine Translation". *For Roman Jakobson*, The Hague, Mouton, 1956, pp. 180-186; see pp. 65-75, below.

can be found, the span of which is not limited to the sentence. To make the distinction clear: a deterministic rule is one which under one ascertainable set of conditions comes up with a *yes* branch, under another set of conditions with a *no* branch; a probabilistic rule is one which bases its decision on a tabulation of a set of factors and branches off into *yes* or *no* depending on relative percentages rather than absolute conditions. Broadly speaking those translation decisions which are based on primarily grammatic conditions — that is, conditions of the co-occurrence of linguistic forms — will be largely deterministic. Decisions that are based on other conditions will be largely probabilistic. It is clear again that in terms of the actual design of a program, deterministic routines should be given precedence over probabilistic ones.

CONTENT PROCESSING

As indicated above, the field of content processing differs from machine translation in that it requires not merely the rendition of the content of the document, but its evaluation according to some relevance criterion. Evaluation in turn implies comparison of elements in terms of this relevance criterion; such a comparison then presupposes some orderly classification within the frame of which units can be selected for their comparability. The principles of classification will be discussed further below.

At several points in the flow of an information-retrieval or automatic abstracting system one may reasonably speak of the processing of the content of natural-language messages. At the input of an information-retrieval system is the user's *request for information*. If this request is phrased in natural language, it will have to be processed for transmittal to the internal phase. Systems in which the request is either stated in some *standardized language* or is reformulated manually, will not require language-data processing at this point.

The internal phase of a retrieval system consists of information from which portions relevant to the request are selected for display at the output end. The ordering system used for the storage of this information can be called a system of *indexing*, since it is comparable in purpose — though not necessarily in structure or efficiency — to the index of a file or library. This indexing system can be prepared manually, in which case only the actual searching operations within the memory are automated; if it is not prepared manually — that is, if the system is equipped for *automatic indexing* — natural language has to be processed. In this case it is the natural language of a series of documents, the informational content of which is to be stored in the memory. Needless to say, systems are possible and have been devised in which neither the formulation of the request in machine language nor the storage in indexed form is done by machine, but such systems — although of unquestioned utility for a number of purposes — are of no interest in the present framework.

Automatic abstracting by the nature of the process uses documents in natural language at the input, and the system must therefore be capable of recognizing content indices in natural-language text in order to yield at the output the required condensed representation.

In all the above it is again possible to divide the automatic process into a recognition phase and a command phase. If this is done it becomes apparent that the automatic processing of the natural language of informational requests, the automatic processing of natural-language documents for indexing, and the automatic processing of natural-language documents for abstracting all fall under the same heading of being recognition operations, with similar requirements for a recognition routine. Where they differ is essentially in their command routines. The command routine for the processing of the informational request will have to include commands for translation into a search language to be used during the search. In automatic indexing the command routine will have to consist of commands for the storage of portions of documents in appropriate memory locations corresponding to the index terms under which they can be retrieved during the search. In automatic abstracting the command routines will have to consist essentially of *accept* and *reject* commands for individual sentences, if — as is the case at the present state of the research — abstracting is in effect an activity of extracting. It is possible that a future automatic abstracting system may be capable of rewording the sentences extracted for retention in the abstract by generating natural-language text on its own in order to approximate more closely human abstracts, which have certain characteristics of continuity and readability that are absent in mere extracts. This particular final phase of automatic abstracting is the one area of language-data processing in which at the present we can visualize a genuine practical way of sentence generation by machine. This is, of course, as yet for the future, but it may turn out to be an important area of application for some of the efforts of linguists today in the formulation of generative grammars.

From the linguist's point of view, the major purpose of language-data processing as discussed above is the recognition of content for purposes of comparative evaluation. The program must ideally be capable of doing two things: it must first recognize an individual *content element* in the natural-language text (a single word or a relevant combination of words); second, it must be able to decide on some comparability criterion for each of the content elements that it has found.

In order to meet the first of these requirements, the program will have to include some features comparable in nature to those of the algorithms used in machine translation. Something like an *idiom routine* is necessary to recognize word combinations that represent single content elements, as well as provisions for the recognition of the syntactic units and relations relevant to the objective. In technical terms, the system must contain a machine dictionary equipped with a grammar code capable of calling appropriate subroutines for idiom lookup and syntactic recognition.

An additional area of the application of syntax routines to content processing has been suggested by one school of linguistics: the automatic standardization of the language of the original document. The purpose of such a set of routines would be to transform all the sentences of a document into sentences of a type exhibiting a maximally desirable structure, namely kernel sentences. The assumption is that storage in this kernelized form will significantly facilitate retrieval.

To meet the second requirement, the dictionary will have to include, in addition to a grammar code, a semantic code capable of calling appropriate subroutines for content comparison and evaluation.

SEMANTIC CLASSIFICATION AND SEMANTIC CODE

In order to compare content elements to each other in terms of some relevance criterion related to the goal of the operation, whether it is processing of the request, assignment to index terms, or acceptance or rejection for the extract, these elements must be classified in terms of the content which they represent, rather than in terms of their formal co-occurrence characteristics. The semantic code will thus have to be able to refer each dictionary entry to the appropriate area of content representation — that is, to the semantic class to which it belongs. For optimal efficiency such a semantic code ought to be based on a systematic classification of content elements. Classifications of a kind can be found in existing thesauri and partial classifications can be found in synonym lists. There are two major defects in thesauri of the Roget type: one is that they usually do not contain enough of the technical terminology required for most practical content-processing purposes; the other, more serious from a linguistic standpoint, is that they are compiled purely intuitively and without adequate empirical controls, sometimes on the basis of an underlying philosophic assumption, and do not necessarily reflect the intrinsic content structure of the language which they represent. Most synonym lists have similar weaknesses.

These criticisms are based on the assumption that there may exist for each language a system of content in the same sense in which there exists the formal system that linguists deal with when they treat the various levels of a language. This assumption is not unreasonable in view of the intuitive observation that the meanings of content elements are not unrelated to each other. It is, after all, from a similar assumption of the systematic relatedness of formal elements that modern descriptive linguistics has derived its results.

It is thus possible to envision a systematization of content, or meaning, not unlike the systematization of linguistic form for which today we have the capability. It is likewise not unreasonable to assume that some of the methods which have allowed us to systematize formal linguistic relations may contribute to a systematization of content relations. The following linguistic considerations have bearing on such a systematization.

First, the basic assumption that there exists for each language a system of meanings comparable to the system of forms allows application of linguistic methods to the problem of meaning.

Second, two methodological assumptions can be made that allow the formulation of linguistic techniques for the treatment of meaning: (1) that, irrespective of theoretical controversies about the "nature" of meaning, there are two kinds of observable and operationally tractable manifestations of linguistic meaning — translation and paraphrase; and (2) that linguistic units with similar meanings will tend to occur in environments characterized by certain specifiable similarities.

The first assumption allows the formulation of techniques for semantic classification based on similarities in the translation or paraphrase of the content-bearing elements in question. In a monolingual approach, which most workers in the area of content processing would consider the only reasonable one, these would be paraphrasing techniques.

The second assumption permits the extension of linguistic techniques of distributional analysis from problems of form to problems of meaning.

In order for either type of linguistic techniques to yield significant and reliable results, the conditions affecting their application will have to be controlled and the appropriate comparison constants specified. If this is done, one may reasonably expect to arrive at a semantic classification of the content-bearing elements of a language which is inductively inferred from the study of text, rather than superimposed from some viewpoint external to the structure of the language. Such a classification can be expected to yield more reliable answers to the problems of synonymity and content representation than the existing thesauri and synonym lists.

Two directions of research can be envisioned at present: the application of a technique of paraphrasing, and the investigation of the role of context in the definition of meaning. Both lines of study can be based on prior linguistic research experience.

The paraphrasing technique can most usefully be applied to the study of the verbal elements of a language such as English. It can be based on the use of replacement predicates, limited in number and of the required semantic generality, which can be substituted for the original verbal elements found in the sample text that is to be processed.

The following example illustrates how such replacement forms can serve to define the potential semantic features of a given original form:

First rephrasing operation

Original statement: The induction and the confirmation of the theory depend on experience.

Original form: depend on

Replacement form: be based on

Resultant statement: The induction and the confirmation of the theory *are based on* experience.

Comparison property: semantic similarity

Semantic feature induced from operation: basic relation

Second rephrasing operation

Original statement: In all other cases, the magnitudes of the elements *m*, *r*, and *t* of the problem depend on the motion of the observer relative to point P_0.

Original form: depend on

Replacement form: vary with

Resultant statement: In all other cases, the magnitudes of the

elements *m, r,* and *t* of the problem *vary with* the motion of the observer relative to point P_0.
Comparison property: semantic similarity
Semantic feature induced from operation: covariance

These operations have yielded a crude first-approximation semantic spectrum of the verbal element *depend on,* which can be represented in a manner suitable for adaptation to a semantic bit-pattern code:

Lexical unit		*Semantic features*	
	basic relation	*constituency*	*covariance ...*
	be based on	consist of	vary with ...
depend on	1	0	1

It is assumed that the successive application of paraphrasing operations to a large sample of text will serve to establish a series of semantic features for each verbal element that has occurred. On the basis of similarities and differences in their respective sets of features, the verbal elements can then be arranged in a systematic thesaurus. Such a thesaurus would have been inductively derived from the processing of text, and thus could be considered empirically more reliable.[9]

Once a thesaurus of verbal elements is available, the nominal elements of the language can be classified semantically on the basis of their co-occurrence with semantic classes of verbal elements. Each nominal element in a text can then be assigned semantic features, depending on whether or not it has been found to occur as the subject or object of members of the various classes in thesaurus. This research can ultimately be automated, but first the detailed requirements for such a program must be worked out.

The application in content processing of such an empirically

[9] For a detailed discussion of this proposed approach, see now Paul L. Garvin, Jocelyn Brewer and Madeleine Mathiot, *Predication-Typing: A Pilot Study in Semantic Analysis* (= *Language Monograph* No. 27) (Linguistic Society of America Baltimore, 1967).

derived systematization of meaning is outlined below as it would apply to information retrieval.

As mentioned above, natural language has to be processed at two points in the flow of an ideal system: the inputting of requests, and the automatic assignment of document content to index terms. The latter further implies the systematic storage of the indexed information, based on a systematization of the terms to which the information has been assigned. The processing of the request, finally, has to be related to the ordering of the stored terms to permit retrieval of pertinent information. Thus, both language-data-processing operations are ultimately referred to the same semantic system. It is possible to envision this semantic system as a set of thesaurus heads and subheads, with the individual content-bearing elements of language classed under the lowest subheads, each of which will include under it a number of elements which for all operational purposes can be considered synonymous.

The semantic classes and subclasses subsumed under the heads and subheads will have been derived inductively by the linguistic techniques suggested above. They will have been based on a finite set of semantic features ascertained by these techniques. These features would be classified so that the broadest classes would be defined by shared features that are few in number and more general in scope, the narrowest subclasses by features that are many in number and more specific.

The criteria on which to base these semantic features and the techniques for ascertaining them could be related even more specifically to the purposes of automatic indexing or abstracting than the techniques described above. In the case of information retrieval it might be reasonable to base equivalences on reference to the same subject-matter area rather than on some simple relation of synonymity based on sameness of content.

The information derived from such an analysis of the semantic system of the language can then be incorporated in the semantic code, which is part of the machine dictionary. In the indexing phase of a retrieval program, the document can be run against the dictionary; the semantic code would then assign its contents to the appropriate index terms, which can be stored in memory in the ordering derived from the semantic system on which the semantic code is based. In the request-reading phase, the request can be run against the dictionary, and the semantic code could serve to extract the index terms by means of which the required information is retrieved from storage and furnished in answers to the request.

In summary, it is worth noting that the major difference between a linguistic and a nonlinguistic approach to content processing is that the former ideally requires the inclusion of a previously prepared machine dictionary with a dual code: a grammar code and semantic code. To offset this added complexity, a linguistic approach should contribute increased accuracy and reliability.

This discussion has been limited to some of the areas of linguistic contribution, both theoretical and methodological. This is not intended to imply that techniques based on nonlinguistic assumptions and approaches, whether statistical, logical, or philosophical, are in any way considered potentially less significant. On the contrary, the rules which may be derived for content processing from a linguistic analysis of content systems might well turn out to be largely probabilistic rather than deterministic in the sense these terms are used in the above discussion of machine translation. If this is so, the linguistic classifications will indeed have to be meaningfully related to the statistical, logical, and other considerations which are now being set forth in other areas of language-data processing.

II

ISSUES

SOME COMMENTS ON ALGORITHM AND GRAMMAR IN THE AUTOMATIC PARSING OF NATURAL LANGUAGES*

1. Two basic approaches can be singled out in the automatic parsing of natural languages. These are here called *bipartite* and *tripartite*, respectively. In the bipartite approach, the parsing program consists of two basic portions: a machine dictionary which contains grammar codes for each entry, and a recognition algorithm based on a grammar of the source language; the grammar is here in fact written into the algorithm. The tripartite approach is based on a strict separation of grammar and algorithm; the parsing program here consists of three basic portions: the machine dictionary with grammar codes, a stored grammar, and a parsing algorithm which utilizes the codes furnished by the dictionary and applies the grammar.

The purpose of this paper is to examine the validity of the frequently repeated contention that the tripartite approach, consisting in the separation of algorithm and grammar, is particularly desirable in automatic-parsing programs. This examination will be restricted to the area of automatic parsing of natural languages with particular attention to the parsing problems encountered in machine translation.

It must be noted at the outset that in this author's opinion the aim of the automatic-parsing component of a machine-translation program is the adequate recognition of the boundaries and functions of syntactic units. On the basis of this recognition, automatic

* Work on this paper was done at The Bunker-Ramo Corporation under the sponsorship of the Information Processing Laboratory of the Rome Air Development Center of the United States Air Force, under Contract AF30(602)-3506. An earlier version of this paper was presented at the 1965 International Conference on Computational Linguistics, New York, May 19-21.

translation on a sentence-by-sentence rather than a word-by-word basis can be effected.

2. The argument in favor of the tripartite approach is roughly the following: many proponents of formal grammar claim that it is possible to construct a single simple parsing algorithm to be used with any of several grammars of a certain type. The type of grammar has to be specified very precisely by means of a grammar-rule format. These grammars can be written in the form of tables of rules, and the same algorithm can be used alternatively with several of these grammar tables, provided the rule format is adhered to. The advantage of this approach is supposed to be greater simplicity and easier checkout and updating of the grammar. This is because the algorithm need not be changed every time a correction is made in the grammar: presumably any such correction will be a simple revision of the grammar table.

3. In assessing the usefulness of the separation of grammar and algorithm, it is important to keep in mind the well-known distinction between context-free and context-sensitive grammars. In this author's frame of reference, this distinction can be formulated very simply as follows: a context-free grammar is one in which only the internal structure of a given construction is taken into account; a context-sensitive one is one in which both the internal structure and the external functioning are taken into account. This view follows from the conception that internal structure and external functioning are two separate, related, but not identical, functional characteristics of the units of language such as syntactic units.

There are two important considerations which follow from this. One is that very often the internal structure of a construction is not adequate to determine its external functioning. The well-known fact must be taken into account that sequences with identical internal structure may have vastly different modes of external functioning and conversely. Examples of this are very common in English and include many of the frequently cited instances of nesting. The second consideration is that the determination of external functioning by context searching is not a simple one-shot operation. It is not always possible to formulate a particular single context for a particular sequence that is to be examined. Rather, the variety of contextual conditions which may apply to a particular construction may differ from sentence to sentence, and the particular conditions that apply can be determined only by a graduated search of a potentially ever extending range of contexts. This means that one cannot simply talk of context-sensitivity in a grammar but one should talk of degrees of context-sensitivity. In order, therefore, to parse natural-language data adequately, the parsing system has to have not merely some fixed capability of being sensitive to a certain range of contexts but a capacity to increase its context-sensitivity.

This means that the most significant alterations in grammar rules from the standpoint of natural-language parsing will not be those that affect the formation of particular rules within the same format. Rather, those alternatives that will really make a difference in the adequacy of the parsings of natural-language sentences will be alterations of the format itself in terms of increasing the degree of context-sensitivity. This in effect means that the simplicity claimed for a separate table of rules with a constant algorithm turns out to be illusory, since the proponents of this concept of simplicity admit that it applies only when the rules are held to the same format.

4. Another point raised in connection with the separation of grammar and algorithm is that the grammar table constitutes a set of input data to the particular algorithm, in a similar way in which the sentences to be parsed constitute input data. In this author's opinion, this is again an oversimplification.

First of all, it is to be noted that, in the view of many programmers, only those data are considered input that are designed to be actually processed. Since the grammar rules are not intended to be subject to processing, but rather to constitute the parameters for processing, they are not input data in any way comparable to the sentences that are to be parsed.

If, on the other hand, the question of processing is to be ignored in deciding what is to be viewed as input data, then another consideration must be taken into account. It is the following: the question as to what constitutes input can not be answered in the absolute, but only relatively. That is, the question is not simply "Is it input?" but "What is it input to?" This means that the answer depends, at least in part, on what portions of the program are previously present in the work space and what additional portions are inputted subsequently. In a bipartite program in which the grammar is written into the algorithm, such as is the case in the approach this author has taken, the question of whether the grammar constitutes input data can then be viewed as follows: while the grammar does not constitute a separate set of input data, it nevertheless will use separate sets of grammatical input data in the form of a grammar-coded dictionary that is fed into the program from a separate source. Likewise, it is possible to view the executive routine of the algorithm which contains the grammar as the actual parsing algorithm and to view the remaining portions as forms of input data.

5. Leaving aside the matters of rule format and input data, two further questions can be raised concerning the simplicity that is claimed to result from the separation of grammar and algorithm. These questions are pertinent in the case of a grammar having sufficient context-sensitivity to serve the needs of syntactic recognition adequate for the machine translation of natural languages.

a) Since the table will tend to be increasingly complex because of the requirement of high context-sensitivity, a dictionary-type binary lookup may no longer be sufficient. Rather, it may become necessary to devise an algorithm for searching the table in such a way that the graduation of contextual conditions is taken into account properly.

b) Revisions of the rules in such a complex table will not be as simple a matter as it seems, because it will no longer be obvious which of the rules is to be modified in a given case, nor will it be obvious where in the table this rule can be found. Likewise, it will not be obvious what contextual conditions will have to be taken into account in order to bring about the desired modification.

6. As can be seen, the argument in favor of the separation of grammar and algorithm is considered far from convincing. It does

raise a related question, however: If the major separation is not to be that between grammar and algorithm, what then are the major components of a parsing program?

The answer which this author has found satisfactory is the well-known one of structuring the parsing program as an executive main routine with appropriate subroutines. This raises the further question of the functions and design of the executive routine and subroutines.

In this type of parsing program, the function of the executive routine will be to determine what units to look for and where to look for them. The aim of the subroutines will be to provide the means for carrying out the necessary searches.

The design principle for such a parsing program will be the well-known one of functional subroutinization: the program will contain a set of self-contained and interchangeable subroutines designed to perform individual functions.

The subroutines will be of two kinds: analytic subroutines, the purpose of which will be to perform tasks of linguistic analysis such as the determination of the internal structure and external functioning of the different constructions that are to be recognized, and housekeeping subroutines, which are to insure that the program is at all times aware of where it stands. The latter means the following: the program has to know what word it is dealing with; the program has to know at each step how far a given search is allowed to go and what points it is not allowed to go beyond; the program has to be informed at all times of the necessary location information, such as sentence boundaries, word positions in the sentence, search distances, etc.

III

DEVELOPMENT

THE GEORGETOWN-IBM EXPERIMENT OF 1954: AN EVALUATION IN RETROSPECT*

Enough time has elapsed and sufficient other work has been attempted in machine translation since 1954 to allow an appraisal of this much-talked-about demonstration in the light of the experience since gained.

Whatever its implications may have been in terms of publicizing and stirring up interest in the problem, from a research standpoint the purpose of the verbal program underlying the Georgetown-IBM experiment of 7 January 1954 was to test the feasibility of machine translation by devising a maximally simple but realistic set of translation rules that were also programmable. The actual execution of the program on the 701 computer turned out to be an interesting exercise in nonmathematical programming, but showed nothing about translation beyond what was already contained in the verbal rules.

The verbal program was simple because the translation algorithm consisted of a few severely limited rules, each containing a simple recognition routine with one or two simple commands. It was realistic because the rules dealt with genuine decision problems, based on the identification of the two fundamental types of translation decisions: selection decisions and arrangement decisions.

The limitations of the translation algorithm were dual: the search span of the recognition routine was restricted to the immediately adjacent item[1] to the left or right; the command routine was

* Work on this paper was done at The Bunkeer-Ramo Corporation under the sponsorship of the AF Office of Scientific Research of the Office of Aerospace Research under Contract No. AF 49 (638) — 1128.

1 The term "item" was introduced to designate Russian words or word partials, as opposed to the term "word" which was reserved for computer words. The term "decision point" was introduced to designate an item for which the

restricted, for selection decisions, to a choice from among two equivalents, for arrangement decisions, to a rearrangement of the translations of two immediately adjacent items.

The translation program was applied to one Russian sentence at a time: the lookup would bring the glossary entries corresponding to the items of the sentence into the working storage, where the algorithm would go into effect.[2]

The requirements of simplicity and realism were reconciled on the basis of an analysis of the logical structure of a few translation problems. The different variables entering into each problem were isolated, and the rules were then designed to deal each with one particular variable, leaving the remaining aspects of the problem unsolved, or giving an arbitrary solution. In a number of cases, for instance, where the correct choice would have required the operation of rules which were not included in this simple program, a translation appropriate to the input sentences was arbitrarily placed into the glossary. The underlying assumption was that additional rules covering this residue could be written later, without invalidating the rules included in the experiment.

Thus, the translation of Russian case suffixes was analyzed into two decision steps: a first-order decision to determine whether or not to translate the suffix by a preposition, and a second-order decision to choose the particular preposition where one is required. In the experiment, only the first-order decision was implemented, and for only a few suffixes; the second-order decision was ignored by arbitrarily assigning a simple English prepositional translation to each suffix (namely, that which impressionistically seemed the most frequent). This was done by applying rule 3: case suffixes with other than accusatival function were translated by zero whenever a Russian preposition or adjectival suffix preceded the item

program has to make a translation decision, the term "decision cue" (or "cue") to designate an item which is considered the relevant condition for making a certain decision.

2 A statement of the verbal program, the transliteration table, an excerpt from the machine glossary, as well as a selection from the original test sentences, are contained in the Appendix.

in question, they were translated by a preposition when this condition did not apply, and in the latter instance, the order of the translations of stem and suffix (the English noun or adjective, and preposition, respectively) was then inverted.

The same rule was used to effect the translation decision for first-person plural forms of verbs, which is analogous to the first-order decision for case suffixes: the verb form was translated without using a pronoun in English whenever a pronoun was present in the Russian text (sentence 32).

Another method of simplifying the translation decision was to limit the cue distance (i.e., the distance between decision cue and decision point) and cue location arbitrarily to conform to the one-word search span, while realistically defining the decision cue in terms of grammatical conditions. An instance of this was the application of rule 3 to the translation of the case suffixes -a, -я. For the appropriate nouns these were interpreted as animate accusatives and translated by zero, whenever they were preceded by a transitive verb form (sentence 40).

A further simplification of certain selection decisions affecting the translation of prepositions, verbs, and nouns, was brought about by not only restricting the cue distance but also limiting the scope of the decision itself to a choice between two equivalents.

Thus, the translation of the preposition к was effected by rule 2 as determined by certain governed nouns, and other aspects of the translation decision were ignored (sentences 4, 19, 40). Conversely, rule 3 was used to translate a noun as determined by the immediately preceding governing verb (sentence 31), or by a modifying adjective (sentences 15-17). The definite article was selected by rule 5 in a few cases in which the Russian noun in question preceded a noun in the genetive, corresponding to the English construction *N of N,* in which an article is frequently required for the first of the two nouns (sentences 19, 20, 27-29).[3]

One arrangement decision in addition to that required for case suffix translation was made: rule 1 was used to invert the order

[3] This solution was suggested by A. A. Hill.

of the translations of a verb and its immediately following subject (sentences 2, 7, 11, 13, 33-34, 45).

Finally, one idiom translation was attempted: rules 3 and 5 were used to translate a three-word Russian idiom by its two-word English equivalent (sentence 26). This was done by choosing the second English word as the equivalent of the second Russian word by rule 5, with the third Russian word considered the cue, and by choosing zero as the equivalent of the third Russian word by rule 3, with the second Russian word considered the cue (for the term "cue", see fn. 2).

The program utilized a dictionary lookup for calling the translation algorithm in the following manner:

The suffixes for which translation decisions were made, and the stems from which they had to be detached, were each entered in the glossary separately. A stem-suffix splitting subroutine, called the "hyphen rule", was included in the lookup. It was applied only to the so-called subdivided items, i.e., the items involved in the above suffix-translation decisions; all other glossary items were entered undivided.

All entries, whether they represented undivided items or the portions of subdivided items, were listed in a single alphabetic sequence.

The five rules of the translation algorithm were operated by a set of two-digit and three-digit numerical code symbols, called diacritics, attached to the glossary entries. The first of the digits was used to indicate whether the diacritic was assigned to a decision-point entry or a decision-cue entry. The second digit indicated the number of the rule to be applied, and the third digit, used only for some decision-cue diacritics, marked which of two choices was to be made (for terms, see fn. 2).

One limitation was imposed by the convenience of the computer program, namely that a particular glossary entry was allowed to contain no more than two three-digit diacritics and one two-digit diacritic.

The general characteristics of the 1954 experiment can be summarized as follows:

(1) The scope of the translation program was clearly specified. Any sentence meeting its narrow specifications could be translated, provided the required entries were present in the glossary. The glossary could be expanded without difficulty and the program made to operate on it, provided the new entries were limited to items to which the previously established code diacritics could be assigned.

(2) The lookup routine was designed for maximum efficiency of the translation algorithm, in that the splitting subroutine was applied only to those cases where it would serve to simplify the operation of the rules, and not to all grammatically possible cases.

(3) The translation algorithm was based on the collocation of decision points and decision cues, rather than directly on the linguistic factors involved, although the decision points and cues themselves were established by linguistic analysis. The same rule was thus used to solve problems of different linguistic structure, but with similar decision structure; rule 3, for instance, was used to translate case suffixes, to choose the translation of nouns on the basis of the verbs governing them, to translate verbs with or without pronouns, and was also utilized in the one idiom translation.

(4) The word length of a sentence turned out to be operationally trivial, since the rules allowed the translation of consecutive strings of similar constructions, provided they were within the specifications of the algorithm.

(5) Selection and arrangement were confirmed as the basic algorithmic operations. "Omission" and "insertion" emerged as as simple variants of the selection problem: omission amounted to the choice of a zero equivalent; insertion to the choice of a two-or-more word equivalent for a single input word.

The importance of the 1954 experiment lies in the fact that it formed a significant first step in a continuing research process which is first now nearing completion. This first step consisted in providing an essentially correct formulation of the problem of machine translation which can be succinctly stated as follows:

(1) The machine translation problem is basically a decision problem.

(2) The two fundamental types of decisions are selection decisions and arrangement decisions.

(3) For the automatic implementation of a translation decision, the algorithm has to have the capability for recognizing the decision points and the appropriate decision cues.

The research derived from this formulation has therefore been focused on the detection of the recognition criteria needed for the identification of the decision points and decision cues. This approach to the decision problem is based on an understanding of syntactic and semantic structure which increases as our empirical treatment of it develops.

APPENDIX: DOCUMENTATION OF THE 1954 EXPERIMENT

1. *Verbal Program*

Lookup

Match each item of the input sentence consecutively against items stored at the head of glossary entries. Apply hyphen rule whenever necessary.

Hyphen rule. If the lookup does not find a match for all the letters of an input item with a complete item in the glossary, try first for a match of the initial letters with a left partial (stem, as indicated in the glossary by a following hyphen), then try for a match of the remaining letters with a right partial (suffix, as indicated in the glossary by a preceding hyphen).

Bring matched glossary entries into working storage in the order of the input.

Algorithm

Calling the rules. Scan the diacritic field of the dictionary entries in working storage consecutively from left to right until you find the first decision-point diacritic, as indicated by a numeral 1 in the first digit position, and operate the rule indicated by the second digit of the diacritic. Then return to scanning for diacritics, beginning with the entry immediately to the right of where you left off.

Rule 1. Look for cue diacritic 21 in the diacritic part of a complete-item entry immediately to the left of the decision point.

Yes — invert the order of the translations of the items concerned.

No — retain order.

Rule 2. If the decision point is a complete item, look for cue diacritics 221 or 222 in the diacritic field of a complete-item entry, or of either partial entry for a subdivided item, immediately to the right of the decision point. If the decision point is a left partial, look for cue diacritics in the corresponding right-partial entry. Select as follows:

221 — choose the first equivalent of the decision-point entry.

222 — choose the second equivalent of the decision-point entry.

Rule 3. If the decision point is a left partial, look for cue diacritic 23 in the diacritic field of a complete-item entry, or of either partial entry for a subdivided item, immediately to the left of the decision point. If the decision point is a right partial, look for cue diacritic 23 in the diacritic field of a corresponding left-partial entry.

Yes — choose the second equivalent of the decision-point entry.

No — choose the first equivalent of the decision-point entry, then invert order as follows: if the decision point is a complete item or a left partial, place its translation before that of the item immediately to the left of it; if the decision point is a right partial, invert the order of the translations of the right and left partials.

Rule 4. Look for cue diacritics 241 or 242 in the diacritic field of a complete-item entry or of either partial entry for a subdivided item, immediately to the left of the decision point. Select as follows:

241 — choose the first equivalent of the decision-point entry.

242 — choose the second equivalent of the decision-point entry.

Rule 5. Look for cue diacritic 25 in the diacritic field of a complete-item entry, or of either partial entry for a subdivided item, immediately to the right of the decision point.

Yes — choose the second equivalent of the decision-point entry.

No — choose the first equivalent of the decision-point entry.

2. *Transliteration table*

А A	Ж ZH	М M	С S	Ц TS	Ь J
Б B	З Z	Н N	Т T	Ч CH	Э E
В V	И YI	О O	У U	Ш SH	Ю YU
Г G	Й Y	П P	Ф F	Щ SHCH	Я YA
Д D	К K	Р R	Х X	Ы I	Ъ W
Е YE	Л L				

3. *Excerpt From Glossary*

ENTRY	EQUIVALENTS	CODES		
-A	OF	131	222	25
	—	132	222	25
-AMYI	BY	131	222	
	—	132	222	
BO-	BATTLE	222		
BOLJSH-	A LARGE			
	LARGE			
BOYETS	FIGHTER	242		
BYENZYIN	GASOLINE	241	21	
BYETON-	CONCRETE			
DLYIN-	LENGTH			
DOBIVAYUT	THEY OBTAIN	110		
DOMA	AT HOME	151	241	
	HOUSES	152	241	
DOROGI	ROADS	241		
DUG-	ARC			
DYINAMYIT	DYNAMITE	241	21	
FAKTOR-	FACTOR			
FYEDYERATSYIYA	A FEDERATION			
	THE FEDERATION			
GRAZHDANSK-	CIVIL			
-I	OF	131	25	
	—	132	25	

ENTRY	EQUIVALENTS	CODES		
-IM	BY	131	23	
	—	132	23	
-IMYI	BY	131	222	23
	—	132	222	23
-IX	OF	131	222	23
	—	132	222	23
-IY	—			
-IYE	—	222		
-JYU	BY	131		
	—	132		
K	TO	121	23	
	FOR	122	23	
KACHYESTVO	QUALITY	151	222	
	THE QUALITY	152	222	
KALORYIYNOST-	CALORY CONTENT			
KALORYIYNOSTJ	CALORY CONTENT			
KAMN-	STONE			
KAMYENN-	STONY	151		
	—	152		
KARTOFYEL-	POTATOES			
KLYINOM	BY A WEDGE	131		
	IN WEDGE FORMATION	132		
KRAXMAL	STARCH	21		
KYIRPYICH-	BRICK			
KYISLORODN-	OXYGEN			
LYISHYENYI-	DEPRIVAL	221		
MATYERYIAL-	MATERIAL			
MI	WE	23		
MISLYI	THOUGHTS			
MNOG-	MANY			
MYEDJ	COPPER	21		
MYEST-	PLACE	151	23	
	SITE	152	23	
MYEXANYICHESK-	MECHANICAL	242		
MYEZHDUNARODN-	INTERNATIONAL			
NA	ON	121	23	
	FOR	122	23	
NAUKA	A SCIENCE	242		
	THE SCIENCE	242		
NYEFT-	CRUDE OIL			
NYITROGLYITSYERYIN-	NITROGLYCERINE			
NYIVYELYIROVANYI-	LEVELING			
O	ABOUT	141	23	
	OF	142	23	
OBRABOTKA	PROCESSING			

ENTRY	EQUIVALENTS	CODES	
-OGO	OF	131	23
	—	132	23
-OM	BY	131	
	—	132	
OPRYEDYELYAYET	DETERMINES		
OPRYEDYELYAYETSYA	IS DETERMINED		
OPTYICHYESK-	OPTICAL		
OTDYEL-	SECTION		
OTDYELYENYIYE	DIVISION	121	242
	SQUAD	122	242
OTNOSHYENYI-	RELATION	151	
	THE RELATION	152	
-OV	OF	131	222
	—	132	222
-OYE	—		
POGOD-	WEATHER		
POLUCHAYET	GETS		
POLYITYICHYESK-	POLITICAL		
PONYIMANYIYE	UNDERSTANDING	242	
POSLYEDN-	LAST		
	LATEST		
POSRYEDSTVOM	BY MEANS OF	23	
POVISHAYET	INCREASES	121	
	IMPROVES	122	
POZDNO	LATE		
PRAV	OF RIGHTS	131	
	RIGHTS	132	
PRAVO	RIGHT	141	242
	LAW	142	242
PROTSYESS-	PROCESS		
PRYI	AT	121	23
	IN	122	23
PRYIGOTOVLYAYETSYA	IS PREPARED	141	
	PREPARES SELF	142	
PRYIGOTOVLYAYUT	THEY PREPARE	110	
PRYIGOVORYIL	SENTENCED	23	
PRYIMYES-	ADMIXTURE		
PSHYENYITS-	WHEAT		
PUT-	PATH	141	
	METHOD	142	
PYERYEDAYEM	WE TRANSMIT	131	
	TRANSMIT	132	
PYERYEDAYET	TRANSMITS		
PYERYEGOVORI	NEGOTIATIONS	110	241
PYERYEMYIRYI-	AN ARMISTICE		
	THE ARMISTICE		

ENTRY	EQUIVALENTS	CODES		
RABOT-	WORK	222		
RADYIOSTANTSYIYA	A RADIO STATION			
	THE RADIO STATION			
RADYIUS-	RADIUS	221		
RINK-	THE MARKET			
RUD-	ORE			
RYECH-	SPEECH			
RYESHYENYI-	SOLUTION	121	221	
	DECISION	122	221	
S	WITH	23		
SHTAT-	STATE	121		
	STATES	122		
SOOBSHCHYENYIYA	COMMUNICATIONS	241		
SOSTOYIT	CONSISTS			
SOYEDYINYENYI-	COMPOUND	121	242	
	COMPOUNDS	122	242	
SPROS-	THE DEMAND			
SPYIRT	ALCOHOL	21		
STROYATSYA	ARE CONSTRUCTED	141	242	25
	LINE UP	142	242	25
STROYITSYA	IS CONSTRUCTED	141	222	23
	LINES UP	142	222	23
SYELITR-	SALTPETER			
SYERZHANT-	A SERGEANT			
	THE SERGEANT			
TOL	T.N.T.	241	21	
TSYEL-	TARGET	131	25	
	—	132	25	
TSYENA	PRICE	151		
	THE PRICE	152		
-U	TO	131		
	—	132		
UGL-	COAL	121	25	
	ANGLE	122	25	
UGOL	ANGLE			
UGOLOVN-	PENAL	242		
UTROM	IN THE MORNING			
V	IN	121	23	
	TO	122	23	
VAZHN-	AN IMPORTANT			
	IMPORTANT			
VIRABATIVAYETSYA	IS PRODUCED			
VIRABATIVAYUT	THEY PRODUCE	110		
VLADYIMYIR	VLADIMIR	241		
VOPROS-	QUESTION	121		
	QUESTIONS	122		

ENTRY	EQUIVALENTS	CODES		
VOYSKA	TROOPS	242		
VOZVISHYENYIYE	ELEVATION			
VYEDUTSYA	ARE CONDUCTED	21		
VYELYICHYINA	MAGNITUDE			
XYIMYI-	CHEMISTRY			
XYIMYICHYESK-	CHEMICAL	242		
-Y	OF	131	222	
	—	132	222	
-YA	OF	131	221	25
	—	132	221	25
YAVLYAYETSYA	APPEARS	141	23	
	CONSTITUTES	142	23	
-YAX	—	222		
-YE	TO	131	221	
	—	132	221	
-YEM	BY	131		
	—	132		
-YI	OF	131	25	
	—	132	25	
-YIM	BY	131	23	
	—	132	23	
-YIX	OF	131	222	23
	—	132	222	23
-YIYE	—	222		
YIZ	OUT OF	23		
YIZMYERYENYI-	MEASUREMENT			
YIZVYESTYIYA	BULLETINS			
-YU	TO	131		
	—	132		
ZAKONODATYELJSTV-	LEGISLATION			
ZHALOVANYIYE	SALARY			
ZHYELYEZO	IRON	21		

4. *Selected Test Sentences*

1. PRYIGOTOVLYAYUT TOL
2. TOL PRYIGOTOVLYAYUT YIZ UGLYA
3. TOL PRYIGOTOVLYAYETSYA YIZ UGLYA
4. BOYETS PRYIGOTOVLYAYETSYA K BOYU
5. KACHYESTVO UGLYA OPRYEDYELYAYETSYA KALORYIYNOSTJYU
6. TOL PRYIGOTOVLYAYETSYA YIZ KAMYENNOGO UGLYA
7. BYENZYIN DOBIVAYUT YIZ NYEFTYI
8. BYENZYIN DOBIVAYETSYA YIZ NYEFTYI
9. AMMONYIT PRYIGOTOVLYAYUT YIZ SYELYITRI

10. AMMONYIT PRYIGOTOVLYAYETSYA YIZ SYELYITRI
11. SPYIRT VIRABATIVAYUT YIZ KARTOFYELYA
12. SPYIRT VIRABATIVAYETSYA YIZ KARTOFYELYA
13. KRAXMAL VIRABATIVAYUT YIZ KARTOFYELYA
14. KRAXMAL VIRABATIVAYETSYA YIZ KARTOFYELYA
15. TOL PRYIGOTOVLYAYETSYA XYIMYICHYESKYIM PUTYEM YIZ KAMYENNOGO UGLYA
16. AMMONYIT PRYIGOTOVLYAYETSYA XYIMYICHYESKYIM PUTYEM YIZ SYELYITRI
17. KRAXMAL VIRABATIVAYETSYA MYEXANYICHYESKYIM PUTYEM YIZ KARTOFYELYA
18. TSYENA KARTOFYELYA OPRYEDYELYAYETSYA RINKOM
19. VYELYICHYINA UGLA OPRYEDYELYAYETSYA OTNOSHYENYIYEM DLYINI DUGYI K RADYIUSU
20. KALORYIYNOSTJ OPRYEDYELYAYET KACHYESTVO UGLYA
21. OBRABOTKA POVISHAYET KACHYESTVO NYEFTYI
22. ZHYELYEZO DOBIVAYETSYA YIZ RUDI
23. MYEDJ DOBIVAYETSYA YIZ RUDI
24. DYINAMYIT PRYIGOTOVLYAYETSYA YIZ NYTROGLYITSYERINA S PRYIMYESJYU YINYERTNOGO MATERYIALA
25. VOZVISHYENYIYE OPRYEDYELYAYETSYA NYIVYELYIROVANYIYEM
26. UGOL MYESTA TSYELYI OPRYEDYELYAYETSYA OPTYICHYESKYIM YIZMYERYENYIYEM
27. TSYENA PSHYENYITSI OPRYEDYELYAYETSYA RINKOM
28. TSYENA PSHYENYITSI OPRYEDYELYAYETSYA SPROSOM
29. TSYENA KARTOFYELYA OPRYEDYELYAYETSYA SPROSOM
30. DOROGI STROYATSYA YIZ KAMNYA
31. VOYSKA STROYATSYA KLYINOM
32. MI PYERYEDAYEM MISLYI POSRYEDSTVOM RYECHYI
33. ZHYELYEZO DOBIVAYUT YIZ RUDI
34. MYEDJ DOBIVAYUT YIZ RUDI
35. ZHYELYEZO DOBIVAYETSYA YIZ RUDI XYIMYICHESKYIM PROTSYESSOM
36. MYEDJ DOBIVAYETSYA YIZ RUDI XYIMYICHYESKYIM PROTSYESSOM
37. DYINAMYIT PRYIGOTOVLYAYETSYA XYIMYICHYESKYIM PUTYEM YIZ NYITROGLYITSYERYINA S PRYIMYESJYU YINYERTNOGO MATYERYIALA
38. DOMA STROYATSYA YIZ KYIRPYICHA
39. DOMA STROYATSYA YIZ BYETONA
40. VOYENNIY SUD PRYIGOVORYIL SYERZHANTA K LYISHYENYIYU GRAZHDANSKYIX PRAV
41. UGOLOVNOYE PRAVO YAVLYAYETSYA VAZHNIM OTDYELOM ZAKONODATYELJSTVA
42. NAUKA O KYISLORODNIX SOYEDYINYENYIYAX YAVLYAYETSYA VAZHNIM OTDYELOM XYIMYIYI

43. VLADYIMYIR YAVLYAYETSYA NA RABOTU POZDNO UTROM
44. MYEZHDUNARODNOYE PONYIMANYIYE YAVLYAYETSYA VAZHNIM FAKTOROM V RYESHYENYIYI POLYITYICHYESKYIX VOPROSOV
45. VYEDUTSYA PYERYEGOVORI O PYERYEMYIRYIYI
46. FYEDYERATSYIYA SOSTOYIT YIZ MNOGYIX SHTATOV
47. RADYIOSTANTSYIYA PYERYEDAYET POSLYEDNYIYE SOOBSHCHYENYIYA O POGODYE
48. RADYIOSTANTSYIYA PYERYEDAYET POSLYEDNYIYE POLYITYICHYESKYIYE YIZVYESTYIYA
49. VLADYIMYIR POLUCHAYET BOLJSHOYE ZHALOVANYIYE

SOME LINGUISTIC PROBLEMS IN MACHINE TRANSLATION : AN EARLY VIEW STILL HELD*

The Georgetown-IBM experiment in machine translation,[1] in which I participated, raised a number of problems of linguistic method and threw light on some important phases of general linguistic theory.

The purpose of machine translation (MT)[2] is to have a logical machine perform a task which so far has been performed by skilled human beings only — that of translation, that is, "the transference of meaning from one patterned set of symbols occurring in a given culture ... into another set of patterned symbols occurring in another culture ...".[3]

Two questions have to be answered before MT can seriously be attempted: (1) what are the discrete steps involved in the process of translation; (2) how can these steps be stated in terms of the modus operandi of logical machines.

The steps in translation can be discovered by a detailed reconstruction of the translation process from a comparison of the original text with its translation, that is, by translation analysis.

The results of the translation analysis, in order to be compatible

* I am indebted to A. C. Reynolds for discussing these problems with me, especially as regards the characteristics of logical machines and programming (see fn. 4). I am of course solely responsible for my argument and conclusions.

1 See "The Georgetown-IBM Experiment of 1954: An Evaluation in Retrospect", pp. 51-64.

2 Standard MT terms are: "source language" and "target language" for the languages from which and into which the translation is made, "input" and "output" for information fed into and received from the machine.

3 L. E. Dostert, "The Georgetown-IBM Experiment", in: William Locke and Donald Booth, eds., *Machine Translation of Languages*, p. 124, Cambridge, Mass., Technology Press; New York, Wiley; London, Chapman & Hall, 1955.

with the modus operandi of logical machines, must be stated explicitly and unequivocally, that is, with each logical step — including the obvious ones — spelled out in detail, and in terms of the yes-no decisions required by the binary operation of electronic circuits.

The above two aspects of MT research — the translation analysis, and the verbal statement of its results in acceptable terms — are the proper concern of the linguist, since they must be based upon a knowledge of the structures of the languages concerned. The third aspect, the translation of the linguist's statements into a detailed program[4] for a particular machine — be it a specially designed translation machine (which, to my knowledge, does not yet exist), or a general-purpose complex logical machine (such as IBM's 701 computer used in the Georgetown-IBM experiment) — is within the scope of the programming specialist with whom the linguist cooperates.

Translation analysis differs from linguistic analysis by both its subject matter and its objective. Instead of a corpus of forms, its data are a set of reconstructed operations. Instead of discovering the pattern underlying the corpus, its purpose is to make possible the duplication of the operations by a logical machine.

Let me now discuss the data of translation analysis — the translation process — in some detail.

The translation process consists essentially of two sets of operations: operations of selection, and operations of arrangement.[5]

The selection operations have to do with finding the suitable equivalent for each unit to be translated; I shall discuss later what these translation units are. The arrangement operations have to do with making sure that the translations of each unit appear in the

[4] "Programming" is the detailed keying of a logical machine for the performance of a required set of consecutive operations.

[5] Cf. Karl Bühler's two levels of organization ("Klassen von Setzungen"), choice of words ("Wortwahl") and sentence structure ("Satzbau"), *Sprachtheorie* (Gustav Fischer, Jena, 1934), p. 73, also Vilém Mathesius' "onomatology" and "syntax", "On some problems of the systematic analysis of Grammar", *TCLP* 6.98 (1936).

output in such an order that the text as a whole is properly translated.

Selection and arrangement are trivial where one-to-one equivalence exists between source and target units, and where the order of units in the source language is identical with the desired order of units in the target language. In such cases, a simple look-up and matching procedure would be sufficient, and the machine would not be required to "make any decisions": the machine could store, in its memory device, units of the source language together with their single equivalents, and a text could be translated by matching each unit of the input against the corresponding source unit in the memory device, and furnishing the equivalent stored next to it in the output, in the same order in which the input was received.

The selection and arrangement operations include decisions when a source unit has more than one possible equivalent in the target language, and when the sequential order of units in the source language is not identical with the desired order of units in the target language. Then the machine, in order to translate adequately, has to make decisions as to which of the several equivalents to select, and decisions as to whether to retain a given order of units or alter it. This means that in addition to look-up and matching, a "decision program" must be included in the MT setup.[6]

Such a decision program has to meet two requirements: it has to enable the machine to recognize the "decision points", that is, the passages of the input text requiring translation decisions, and it has to furnish the "decision instructions" enabling the machine to execute the correct decisions.

To provide the information on which such a dual decision program can be based is the crucial objective of translation ana-

[6] It is, of course, possible to design a simple dictionary program in which the machine merely furnishes the one or several equivalents of each input unit from its memory in the order of the original text, to be worked into a viable translation by a knowledgeable human editor. Such a "mechanical dictionary" has been talked about in the MT discussion, but the Georgetown-IBM experiment was designed to test the feasibility of MT without either "pre-editing" or "post-editing" (Dostert, *op.cit.*, p. 134).

lysis. Translation analysis can achieve this objective to the extent to which it can establish the predictability of translation decisions in terms of the structural features of the source and target languages, and of the functional properties of language in general.

What, then, is the extent and nature of this predictability? Let me discuss the matter first in regard to selection decisions, and then in regard to arrangement decisions.

Selection decisions in translation concern meaning equivalence; to establish the conditions for the selection of a given equivalent, the various aspects of meaning involved here must be sorted out.

Every unit in the source language can be assumed to have a system-derived general lexical meaning[7] proper to itself. Let me define my terms: by system-derived meaning I mean that range of meaning which is proper to a linguistic unit by virtue of its place in a system of comparable units (in practice, the component of meaning recurrent in all of its distributions); by general meaning I refer to the total of this range of meaning, not merely to the most common and obvious segment of the range; by lexical meaning I designate the meaning uniquely proper to the given unit and not shared by any other unit in the system.

Every unit in the target language must then likewise be assumed to have a system-derived general lexical meaning proper to itself. Since by definition two languages constitute two different systems, the range of meaning of no unit in one can be assumed to coincide exactly with that of a corresponding unit in the other.

This incomplete coincidence of system-derived ranges of meaning is the causative factor in the problem of selection: the range of meaning of a unit in the source language may include pieces of the range of meaning of several units in the target language, the result of which are the multiple equivalents referred to above. The scope of the problem varies for different areas of the lexicon:

[7] The subsequent discussion is partly based on Karl Bühler's concepts of "feldfremd" (= system-derived) and "feldeigen" (= field-derived) (*Sprachtheorie*, p. 183), and on Roman Jakobson's treatment of general meaning and basic meaning, "Zur Struktur des russischen Verbums", *Charisteria Guilelmo Mathesio ... oblata* (Prague, 1932), pp. 74 ff., and "Beitrag zur allgemeinen Kasuslehre", *TCLP* 6.240 ff. (1936).

in colloquial or literary vocabulary there is usually much less coincidence than in technical vocabulary. Much of the latter is derived from the same international urban culture and therefore has reference to a similarly structured cultural reality, it furthermore has the relative exactness of reference required by the "intellectualization" of the standard language in technical and scientific discourse,[8] hence closer coincidence of the ranges of meaning can be expected. The selection problem can on this level be further reduced, thought not completely eliminated, by more refined lexicography: most bilingual dictionaries, for instance, list more equivalents than would be necessary with a more careful matching of ranges of meaning (not to mention that equivalents are often poorly chosen).

The selection problem can then be rephrased as follows: what portion of the total system-derived meaning of the source unit applies in any given textual fragment, and to which of the possible equivalent portions of target units does it correspond?

The answer lies in considering the relationship between the linguistic unit and its environment. By virtue of its place in a system, every linguistic unit "brings with it" into each environment a system-derived range of meaning. This range of meaning is postulated to be relatively wide and relatively vague, since in practice it has to be abstracted from a multitude of environments, and has its value only by virtue of its opposition to other comparable units. The system-derived meaning is in every linguistic context and extralinguistic situation interpreted by the receiver in terms of this environment, and this reinterpretation — essentially a narrowing and specification of the system-derived meaning — can, in Karl Bühler's term (see fn. 7), be called field-derived meaning, in turn consisting of a contextually derived and a situationally derived component.

What is found in a particular text to be translated is thus not

[8] For a discussion of this concept, see B. Havránek in *Spisovná čeština a jazyková kultura* (Prague, 1932), pp. 45-52, translated in *A Prague School Reader on Esthetics, Literary Structure, and Style*, ed. and transl. by Paul L. Garvin, pp. 6-9, Washington, D. C., Georgetown University Press, 1964.

the system-derived meaning as a whole, but that part of it which is included in the contextually and situationally derived meaning proper to the text in question. The equivalents of the total system-derived range of meaning can then be selected in terms of the applicable contextually and situationally derived portions of that range.

Selection decisions are thus, in terms of the above, contextually determined and situationally determined, and the objective of translation analysis becomes one of singling out the specific determining factors for each decision in the given context and situation.

This raises the extremely important problem of the boundary line between linguistic context and extralinguistic situation, since it is difficult if not impossible to envision a logical machine capable of extracting information from the multistructured extralinguistic environment of a text. It is obvious that all nonlinguistic phenomena accompanying a textual unit are part of the extralinguistic situation; this does not, however, imply the converse, namely that all linguistic material accompanying the textual unit is part of the linguistic context in a technical, that is, operationally useful sense. On the contrary, the distinction between linguistic and extralinguistic environment is functionally relevant only if it is made, not in terms of the substantive nature of the environmental material, but in terms of the relationship of this material to the textual unit under consideration. That is, the distinction must be made between environmental material linguistically related to the unit under consideration, and material not so related, whether it is substantively extralinguistic or not. This means that only a certain portion of the linguistic material accompanying a given textual unit can be considered its linguistic context in the technical sense; the remaining linguistic material, together with the extralinguistic material, technically is included in the extralinguistic situation.

Thus, the linguistic context can be defined specifically as all those textual units (i.e., linguistic material) that stand in a linguistic relation to the unit under consideration. A linguistic relation, to be meaningfully distinguishable from a non-linguistic relation in this connection, is defined as a necessary syntagmatic dependence.[9] The boundary line of the linguistic context then becomes the sentence, since the latter can be defined as a syntagmatically self-contained unit.[10]

Summing up the foregoing, the selection decision consists in singling out, within the total system-derived range of meaning of a unit, that portion of the range which applies to the environment in which the unit occurs, and in giving the translation equivalent corresponding to this range. That portion of the environment which qualifies as linguistic context is amenable to machine programming (since all necessary syntagmatic dependences can presumably be formulated in programmable terms), that portion which — whether of linguistic substance of not — has to be classed as the extralinguistic situation is not amenable to programming, since the relations linking this part of the environment to the textual unit in question include too many variables to be manipulable in the required precise terms.

Thus, the extent of machine translatability is limited by the amount of information contained within the same sentence, as defined above.[11]

Arrangement decisions in translation concern the equivalence of sequential relations — the objective of an arrangement decision is to arrive at an order relationship in the output functionally equivalent to that of the input, as a result of which the original order is either retained or altered. To establish the conditions for this retention or alteration of order, the functions of the various sequential order relations in the source and target languages have to be established and compared.

9 Syntagmatic is here used in the sense proposed by André Martinet, namely in reference to relations within the same text. Dependence is used in the Hjelmslevian sense, as discussed in my "Delimitation of Syntactic Units", *Language* 30.346-7 (1954).

10 See my definition of the sentence in Ponapean as one of several mutually tolerant units, *op. cit.*, p. 347.

11 Note that later work has shown that machine translatability can be extended beyond the bounds of the sentence (see pp. 30-31).

We are thus again dealing with problems of meaning equivalence, but instead of the meanings of units we deal with the meanings of relationships, and instead of lexical meaning we are dealing with grammatical meaning, that is, meaning not unique to each given unit but shared by more than one unit. While selection decisions are thus unique and specific to each unit, arrangement decisions are recurrent for classes of units.

Since, however, ranges of grammatical meaning can no more be expected to coincide from one language to another than can ranges of lexical meaning, every arrangement decision contains within its scope a possible selection subdecision, determining which of several alternative sequential order relations is to be executed.

What has been said about the contextually derived and situationally derived determination of selection decisions holds equally, of course, for the selection subdecision within the arrangement decision, although we may for all practical purposes assume that since grammatical meanings are linked to grammatical patterns, contextual determination will here far outweight situational determination. We may furthermore extend the scope of this contextual determination to cover the entire reach of the arrangement decision, not merely its selection aspect.

The above means that, unlike selection decisions, arrangement decisions can — at least as far as the purely linguistic factors are concerned — be considered entirely within the bounds of machine translatability, since the limits of the linguistic context need not be exceeded.

So far, I have discussed the matter only in terms of the operations involved in the translation process, without analyzing the translation units that are manipulated in these operations.

Let me now turn to translation units.

This part of the MT problem area concerns not only the translation units themselves, but also the very crucial problem of the relationship of translation units to sensing units, that is, the kind of units which a logical machine is capable of sensing.[12]

[12] Sensing is the handling of the input data by the machine.

I shall therefore discuss the properties of translation units and attempt to relate them to the corresponding characteristics of sensing units.

First of all, translation units are linguistic units, that is, they are recurrent partials which can be separated out from a text by procedures of linguistic segmentation. Linguistic segmentation — as has lately been discussed in the literature[13] — is based on criteria of both form and meaning; sensing, on the other hand, occurs in terms of form (i.e., physical impulses) alone. This means that where homonyms or homographs, for instance, constitute separate linguistic units (and hence separate translation units), all formally identical homonyms constitute one and the same sensing units, resulting in an additional selection problem.

Secondly, although translation units qua linguistic units are discrete, their physical manifestation need not be discrete. That is, while printed matter, for instance, is composed of discrete letters, speech or handwriting is at least in part continuous, with the physical continuum being interrupted only at some of the linguistically present unit boundaries. In order to sense speech or handwriting, a machine would have to be equipped with an elaborate resolving device capable of breaking up the continuous portions of the physical phenomenon into discrete units. Even then, at the present state of engineering, such a device can only accomodate constant continua, but not variable continua such as normal speech or handwriting.[14] This means that the input of MT, to be practicable in the foreseeable future, will have to be limited to print or some other physically discrete source.

Third is the key problem of the respective extension of sensing units and translation units.

Let me elaborate. Sensing occurs in simple linear progression. For purposes of MT, a machine can be programmed to sense one letter at a time, and to recognize spaces as word boundaries — individual printed words separated by spaces will thus become

[13] For the most recent discussion of this problem, see Henri Frei, "Critères de délimitation", *Word* 10.136-45 (1954).

[14] This assertion is based on a statement of current engineering opinion. See also pp. 18-23

the sensing units[15] which can be matched against comparable units stored in the memory.

In terms of the translation operations applied to the input, however, one printed word separated by spaces does not necessarily constitute a single translation unit. The translation unit — be it a selection unit or an arrangement unit — may consist of one word, or of less than one word, or of more than one word, depending on how much of the text is subject to a given operation at a given time. Thus, there is no one-to-one correspondence between sensing units and translation units, and additional programming has to be introduced to convert sensing units into translation units.

To determine the specific size of translation units, a text must be subjected to linguistic segmentation in much the same way as in determining the extension of any linguistic unit: defining criteria for each type of unit have to be formulated, such that the application of these criteria will result in an exhaustive segmentation of the text into units of that type.

Translation units, as was intimated above, are of two types, in terms of the two types of translation operations: selection units and arrangement units. In operational terms, they can be defined as follows: a selection unit is a unit, the total translation of which is not the sum of the translations of its parts; an arrangement unit is one which, as a whole, occupies a certain sequential order position and the translation of which, as a whole, is subject to a possible shift in sequential order position. In linguistic terms, selection units correspond to lexical units, arrangement units correspond to morphemic[16] units, defined as follows: lexical units are units, the meaning of which is not predictable from the meanings of component units (if such can be segmented out); morphemic units are units, the distribution of which can not be stated in terms of component units (if such can be segmented out). Both

[15] I am disregarding punctuation marks as possible sensing unit boundary markers, since the problem of varying extension is of the same order for such larger units as might be delimited by punctuation marks, and the subsequent discussion, mutatis mutandis, therefore applies to them as well.

[16] Note that in my frame of reference morphemics includes both morphology and syntax. For a succinct presentation of this frame, see pp. 90-93.

lexical and morphemic units may consist of one or more linear segments such as morphemes or words; their internal structure is irrelevant from the standpoint of their meaning or distribution as wholes (or, in MT terms, from the standpoint of the selection and arrangement of their equivalents in translation).

In summary, the properties of translation units (shared in a broader sense by linguistic units in general) contrast with those of sensing units as follows:

(1) translation units are defined by both form and meaning, sensing units are defined by form only;

(2) translation units can be manifested in a variable continuous physical substance,[17] sensing units only in a discrete, or perhaps a constant continuous, substance;

(3) translation units can not be segmented in simple linear progression, sensing units can be sensed only in simple linear progression.

I have tried in the above to formulate some of the considerations which, as a linguist, I regard as basic to MT. They are founded on some assumptions about the functioning and properties of linguistic systems which are inferential in nature, since after all only the noises of speech or their graphic representation (la parole) are directly observable, but not the underlying structure (la langue).

Machine translation involves, in essence, the designing of a machine analog to the postulated resultant of the interaction of two linguistic systems — it will thus allow an instrumental verification of the theoretical assumptions about the nature of these systems and the nature of their interaction, such as the postulated relational difference between the linguistic and the extralinguistic, and the postulated non-linearity of linguistic units.

As a by-product, the requirement of explicitly and unequivocally formulated statements acceptable for programming purposes, will contribute to the rigor and scientific logic of linguistic analysis.

[17] Louis Hjelmslev, *Prolegomena to a Theory of Language*, Francis J. Whitfield, transl. (= *IUPAL Memoir* No. 7, Baltimore, 1953), p. 50.

MACHINE TRANSLATION : A REPORT TO THE VIII INTERNATIONAL CONGRESS OF LINGUISTS

Machine translation is an extremely new field of research. It is only 8 years ago that the idea was formulated by Warren Weaver,[1] and hardly more than five years ago that work on the problem was developed in an organized manner.[2] It is therefore rather difficult to look at MT with complete objectivity and in perspective; I shall, as far as possible, present the problems in the field as I see them and attempt to avoid evaluative criticism.

The term "machine translation" is self-explanatory. I prefer it the earlier term "mechanical translation" because of the ambiguous connotations of that adjective; the Russians[3] use the term "automatic translation". The machine which is expected to perform translation is a logical machine; either a high-speed, high-capacity general-purpose computer, or a machine especially designed for the purpose. The translation which is to be performed by the machine is, certainly for the present, intended to be of technical and scientific texts only, in view of the obvious additional complexities presented by, for instance, colloquial or literary texts.

Machine translation problems can be discussed in terms of the two components of the term: machine problems, and translation problems. Let me follow this breakdown in my discussion.

[1] Translation, a memorandum written by Warren Weaver on 15 July 1949, reprinted in: William N. Locke and A. Donald Booth, eds., *Machine Translation of Languages*, pp. 15-23 (The Technology Press of the Massachusetts Institute of Technology, John Wiley & Sons, New York, Chapman & Hall, London, 1955).

[2] The MIT Conference on Machine Translation, June, 1952, and the Discussion Meeting on MT at the 7th International Congress of Linguists, London, September, 1952.

[3] and the French.

A logical machine, in order to translate, has to perform the following sets of operations: it has to read the input text in the source language, it has to manipulate the input translationally, and it has to furnish a usable output in the target language.

Reading the input and furnishing the output as machine operations are not fundamentally different from the input and output operations that a logical machine has to perform in handling any problem: since most digital computers operate with binary digits, the input operation has to include a transposition of the properly formulated source data into binary code, and the output operation includes the transposition of the binary result into more common symbols (decimal numerals and/or letters). The output can easily be equipped with a printer, resulting in legible printed text — this is common in modern computers, and hence no new equipment is required even for the ultimately contemplated translation program.

The input of modern computers consists of previously prepared punched cards, punched tape, magnetic tape, or the like. This requires preparatory equipment, such as a card punch or tape punch, which has to be operated manually. For a translation program, this means that a human operator has to read the source text and, say, punch it on cards or tape, before it can be fed into the input proper of the machine. In order to eliminate this preparatory human operation, the input of the machine would have to be equipped with an electronic scanning device, optical or acoustic, capable of reading printed text or perceiving speech sounds, and transposing them directly into binary code. At the present time, only the beginnings exist of either a visual or auditory scanner, and the technological difficulties are considerable, in view of the need for separating the relevant from the redundant features of the printed or acoustic stimulus by a machine analog of graphemic or phonemic analysis. Thus, machine translating input will in the immediate future have to be prepared by a human operator, in the same way in which input for any computer operation is now prepared. This input preparation does, however, not in any way constitute a preliminary editing of the text, but is a simple secretarial job, equivalent to retyping.

The machine manipulation of the text fundamentally involves two types of computer operations: table-lookup and algorithmic (that is, properly computative) operations.[4] The table-lookup operation consists in matching the sensed (that is, machine-read) input or certain stored data against a table or tables stored in the memory unit(s) of the machine, and delivering the data from the table(s) to the arithmetic unit(s) of the machine for algorithmic processing. The result of this processing is the translated output, which is then fed into the printer and delivered to the user.

The ratio of table lookup to algorithmic operations will depend on the type of translation program prepared; it seems that modern computers are, or can be made to be, capable of performing either, and thus there are no foreseeable machine limitations on the choice of translation program. In an impressionistic way, it can be asserted that table lookup and algorithmic operations will always be in a roughly inverse proportion. Whether this impression can be technically validated, that is, whether an emphasis on table lookup will reduce algorithmic operations or *vice versa*, only detailed programming research will tell.

From the standpoint of machine design, the table-lookup operation requires extensive memory storage capacity with very rapid access. It is quite obvious that, in any type of translation program, some kind of bilingual dictionary will have to be stored in the machine memory; in order to allow more than trivial translatability, a dictionary of considerable size will have to be contemplated. It is equally obvious that in any translation program input units will have to be matched one after the other in rapid succession against the units contained in the stored glossary. The rapid-access storage requirements of machine translation are far in excess of those required in current mathematical and logical computations; in the latter, extensive storage may be required, but without rapid random access. Bulk data, when required, are usually of the sort

[4] Gilbert King, "The Requirements of Lexical Storage", in: *Report of the Eighth Annual Round Table on Linguistics and Language Teaching, Georgetown University Monographs on Linguistics and Language Teaching* 10: 79-81 (1957).

that can be fed into the machine consecutively from, say, a storage tape.

Technologically then, the problem is not the extent of storage but the requirement that any unit stored in the extensive memory be available for immediate lookup. At the present time, extensive storage is possible economically on devices with slow access; rapid-access memory devices are as yet of somewhat limited capacity. Research is, however, progressing extremely rapidly in this field, and it is quite thinkable that by the time an extensive translation program has been devised, a memory device will exist which can meet the requirements of the program adequately.

Regarding the algorithmic part of a translation program, the major difficulty lies in the fact that the algorithmic requirements of a translation operation are rather different from those of the mathematical and logical operations which modern computers are built to perform. The instructional details for which computer circuits are designed at present require long chains of addition, subtraction, shift and similar operations in order to accomplish what, for translation purposes, could be a single operation. Present-day translation programming, though already demonstrated to be feasible, is exceedingly cumbersome. A translation machine proper thus might contain algorithmic units rather different in design from the arithmetic units now in use in digital computers. Such an alteration in design presents no radical engineering problem, but can certainly not be undertaken until translation programming research has been advanced to the point where a detailed routine has been stabilized to such an extent that no radical changes due to further research can be anticipated, and engineers can begin to design circuits without having to fear a revocation of specifications once given. Engineering opinion here on the whole agrees with linguistic opinion that the translation program has to be formulated first, before any problems of machine design can be attacked realistically.[5]

[5] I gather as much from discussions with Dan A. Belmore, Programming Consultant to the Georgetown MT Project, and from comments by computer engineers visiting the MT seminar at Georgetown.

A translation program, to be successful, has to accomplish more than merely the one-by-one transfer of units from the source language into the target language. It has to include some solution to the problems of choice implicit in the fact that (a) a unit in the source language may have more than one possible equivalent in the target language, and (b) that the order of source-language units in the input may not be suitable for the output in the target language. I have discussed these problems in some detail elsewhere under the headings of selection and arrangement;[6] the gist of the discussion is that the required selection and arrangement decisions can be programmed only if the contextual conditions can be determined under which any given decision from among several possible ones is to be implemented. The linguist's major contribution to MT research consists in the discovery of these conditions, and in the formulation of a routine for basing a decision on it.

There appears to be a certain correlation, on the one hand between lexical conditions and selection decisions, and on the other hand between syntactic conditions and arrangement decisions, but it is by no means to be assumed that selection decisions are based on lexical conditions only, nor that arrangement decisions are based on syntactic — or, more generally, grammatical — conditions only. One of the first results of my own research in MT has been that translation decisions cut across the various levels of linguistic analysis. On the one hand, the same decision may be based on a mixed set of conditions in the source and target languages: lexical, morphological, and syntactic. On the other hand, a given set of conditions — though assignable to one linguistic level only — may require both a selection and an arrangement decision.

A generally accepted example of the above is the translation of'a Russian case suffix by one of several possible English prepositions. The translation of the case suffix separately from the base to which it is attached can be assigned to a set of morphological conditions in the source language; the choice from among several prepositions can be termed a lexical choice; the necessary rearran-

[6] See pp. 66-72.

gement of the order of the translations of the base by an English noun, and of the suffix by a preposition, can be said to result from syntactic conditions in the target language. Thus, for this particular translation situation, there exists a mixed set of conditions — lexical, morphological, and syntactic, and both a selection and an arrangement decision are required in a single routine.

Of particular interest to linguists, as well as a source of a good deal of discussion in the MT field, is whether all linguistic conditions have to be accounted for before a given translation decision can be made. My own opinion is that only some of these conditions are translationally relevant, and that one of the by-products of MT research will be a relevance scale of linguistic factors in terms of their effect on translation decisions.

Once the conditions for a given translation decision (or a set of conjoint decisions) have been ascertained, a routine must be formulated to recognize the appropriate conditions and to implement the required decision; the formulation must be logically flawless in order to allow for programming for a given existing computer, or for a yet-to-be-built translation machine.

As I visualize it in terms of my own experience, the first part of such a translation routine is a recognition routine: the place in the text requiring a decision (that is, the decision point) must be recognized as such, and subsequent to it the conditions for the choice of the appropriate decision (the decision cue or cues) must be found. The recognition routine is then followed by the implementation routine: selection and/or arrangement at the decision point are effected in terms of the decision cue(s).

Of the two routines above, I consider the recognition routine more difficult to formulate (and more fundamental), since a logical machine can not be expected to operate in terms of linguistic instructions (such as 'find the noun in the nominative', or 'if no verb is present'). A code must therefore be devised which, based on linguistic information, allows the recognition of decision points and cues by the type of instructions proper to a logical machine (such as 'if *A* is present, implement decision *X*, if not, implement decision *Y*'). The potential decision points and cues in the source language must thus be provided with appropriate code diacritics, and the code must be stored together with the source units to be matched and with the target units to be channeled into the output.

The formulation of a translation routine must thus include data of the required logical precision for the programming of the following: the source units to be matched against the input, the target unit(s) corresponding to each source unit, the necessary decision point and cue recognition code, and the implementation instructions required to effect the needed decisions on the basis of the recognition routines. All the above data must be stored in the appropriate memory compartments of the machine in order to bring about the necessary manipulation between input and output; the specific apportionment of storage space for this information depends on the technology of the particular machine used, and is therefore no longer part of the formulation but of the machine program itself.

SYNTACTIC RETRIEVAL : A FIRST APPROXIMATION TO OPERATIONAL MACHINE TRANSLATION

Let me state briefly that in my opinion the major purpose of a syntax routine in machine translation is to recognize and appropriately record the boundaries and functions of the various components of the sentence. This syntactic information is not only essential for the efficient solution of the problem of word order for the output, but is equally indispensable for the proper recognition of the determiners for multiple-meaning choices.

It is further becoming increasingly apparent in the work in which I am participating that it is the design of the syntax routine which governs the over-all layout of a good machine translation program and lends it the unity without which it would remain a patchwork of individual subroutines and piecemeal instructions. The conception of syntax thus becomes important beyond the immediate objectives which the routine serves in the program.

In the present paper, I should like to set forth some of the linguistic basic assumptions underlying my own approach to syntax, and some of the design features of the syntax routines that have been and are being developed from it.

My conception of linguistic structure, insofar as it concerns syntax, is comparable to what has become known as the "immediate-constituent model", but with some significant differences. Where the immediate-constituent approach takes the maximum unit — the sentence — as its point of departure and considers its step-by-step breakdown into components of an increasingly lower order of complexity, I prefer to start out with the minimum unit — the morpheme in straight linguistic analysis, the typographical word in language-data processing — and consider its gradual fusion into units of increasingly higher orders of complexity, which I call fused units. A sentence is thus conceived of, not as a simple succession of linear components, but as a compound chain of fused units of different orders of complexity variously encapsulated in each other. Syntactic analysis, including the automatic analysis which an MT syntax routine must perform, then has as its objective the identification of this encapsulation of fused units by ascertaining their boundaries and functions.

The fused-unit approach is particularly well suited to language-data processing, since the minimum units — for this purpose the typographical words — constitute the primarily given sensing units from which the program computes the fused units and their interrelations. The methodological basis for this computation is what I have called the *fulcrum approach* to syntax.

The fulcrum approach is based on the conceptualization of fused units as exhibiting the separate properties of internal structure and external functioning respectively. Internal structure is here defined as the constituency of a fused unit in terms of units of a lower order; external functioning is defined in terms of the relations of a fused unit to units of the same order, together with which it enters into the make up of units of a higher order.

The concept of the fulcrum itself stems from the consistent observation that the various components of a fused unit have differential grammatical information content: one of them, the fulcrum, may be expected to be more informative than the remaining components about the properties of the unit of which it forms part. By using the fulcrum of each unit as a point of departure, its identification as to internal structure (and hence boundaries) and external functioning can be achieved more accurately and completely. By tying together fused units of different orders through their fulcra, the syntax program can acquire the hierarchic organization and unity desirable for maximum flexibility.

Let me give an example.

The fulcrum of a main clause in Russian is its predicate. Why the predicate rather than the subject or a complement is chosen as the fulcrum becomes clear if one considers the relative amount of information that each of these three clause members gives about the other two and hence the clause as a whole.

If the predicate of a clause is known, the agreement characteristics of the predicate, such as number and in certain cases gender, allow a reasonable prediction as to a permissible subject, and its government characteristics allow a reasonable prediction as to permissible complements. A predicate thus allows a reasonable prediction with regard to both remaining clause members.

A nominal block (that is, the MT analog of a nominal phrase), on the other hand, will at best allow a partial prediction as to one of the two remaining major clause members: if its agreement characteristics as to case unambiguously mark it as subject, then its agreement characteristics as to number and gender will allow the assumption of a predicate in the plural if the nominal block is in the plural; but will allow a predicate in either the singular or the plural if the nominal block is in the singular, since the latter may be one of a string of blocks which together may permit a predicate in either number. No further predictions are possible from knowing a nominal block by itself: if its case-agreement characteristics mark it as a non-subject, it still does not follow that it is a complement, since it may be governed by non-predicative material or not subject to government at all; its government characteristics will allow an extension of the block but will not yield further information about the remaining major clause members.

The identification of the fulcra of units of lower orders is by comparison more obvious: the fulcrum of a nominal block is the noun; the fulcrum of a prepositional block is the preposition, since it allows the prediction of the case-agreement characteristics of the nominal block governed by it, etc.

A syntactic retrieval routine based on the fulcrum approach will first identify the fulcrum of a given fused unit and then use it as the initial point from which to retrieve the boundary and function information required for the continued operation of the program. The identification of the fulcrum is made possible by incorporating the relevant information in the grammar code of the words stored in the dictionary.

Identification of the fulcrum presupposes a grammar code organized in terms of the potential syntactic functioning of the words rather than in terms of their morphological origin. This is particularly significant in this connection as regards the indication of word class membership.

Thus, all words that may unambiguously function as predicates are given the same word-class designation in the grammar code — that of predicatives. This includes not only finite verb forms but also unambiguous predicative adjectives and certain other words. Conversely, the different forms of words that are traditionally considered the same part of speech are assigned different word-class membership if they have different syntactic function. Thus, the various forms of a verb are coded for word class as follows: finite verb forms, as mentioned above, are coded as predicatives; infinitives and gerunds are coded as separate word classes; participles are coded as "governing modifiers" together with certain adjectives which have government properties similar to those of participles.

To find a fulcrum, the program will read the word-class field of the grammar code of each word that the lookup has brought forth. If the word is of a class that functions as the fulcrum of a fused unit of a particular type, this information serves as the signal to call the subroutine designed to identify the boundaries and potential function of the unit in question.

The dependence on the grammar code for the initial identification of fulcra implies that this initial search must be limited to one-word fulcra. Since it is impressionistically obvious that not all fused units will have one-word fulcra — particularly, units of a higher order can be expected to have fulcra that are themselves fused units — the program will have to include provisions for the recognition of the boundaries and functions of multiword fulcra based upon the prior identification of their components, beginning with the initial identification of relevant one-word fulcra. This in turn implies, and is closely related to, the over-all problem of the order in which the fulcra of the fused units of different orders are to be identified, so that the sequence in which the search for the various fused units is conducted leads to the correct recognition of their encapsulation.

Rather than attempting a consecutive left-to-right solution of this set of problems, the syntax routines conceived in terms of the fulcrum approach have attacked it by a consecutive series of passes at the sentence, each pass designed to identify fused units of a particular order and type. The advantage of this pass method over a single consecutive left-to-right search is, in my opinion, that, instead of having to account for each of the many possibilities at each step of the left-to-right progression, every pass is limited to a particular syntactic retrieval operation and only information relevant to it has to be carried along during that particular search. With the proper sequencing of passes, the syntactic retrieval problems presented by each sentence can be solved in the order of their magnitude, rather than in the accidental order of their appearance in the text.

In a program based on the pass method, each individual pass is laid out in terms of the information available when the pass is initiated, and in terms of the objective that the pass is intended to accomplish. These two factors are closely related to each other, in that the output of a preceding pass becomes the input of the subsequent pass. The scope of each pass and the order of the various passes thus together present the most significant design problem of the program.

The linguistic considerations entering into this design problem stem from the differential relevance to the over-all structure of the sentence of the various orders of units and their relations. Viewed in terms of the ultimate aim of the program in regard to syntactic resolution, which is the capability for rearranging the order of the major sentence components (that is, subjects, predicates, and complements), the relations between these components become the focal point around which the remaining syntactic relations can be said to be centered.

When this is applied to the organization of the passes, it means that the main syntax pass — that is, the pass designed to identify the boundaries and functions of the major clause members of the main clause — becomes the pivot of the program. The remaining passes can be laid out in terms of the input requirements and expected output of this central pass. Preceding it will be preliminary passes designed to assign grammar codes to words which are not in the dictionary (a missing-word routine), and to aberrant typographical matter such as symbols and formulae, as well as passes designed to compute the information needed as input to the main syntax pass from the information available to the program through the grammar code. Following the main syntax pass will be clean-up passes, the function of which is to fill the gaps in syntactic information remaining after the main syntax pass has accomplished its objective.

Let me now discuss the function of the preliminary passes required by the discrepancy between the information contained in the grammar code and the information necessary for the main syntax pass.

The grammar code furnishes three sets of indications: word-class membership, agreement characteristics, and government characteristics. As is well known, for each dictionary entry, some of this information will be unambiguous, some ambiguous, depending on the particular word forms involved.

Aside from accidental typographical homonyms (such as есть = 'is' or 'eat'), grammatical ambiguities relate to word-class membership and agreement characteristics; where ambiguities as to government characteristics were found, they were dependent an another grammatical function, that of word-class membership.

While the main syntax pass may tolerate agreement ambiguities (although it is not always the most efficient place in the program for their resolution), it can not admit word-class ambiguities in its input, since the fulcrum approach is based on the recognition of the fulcra by their word-class membership. One of the essential functions of the preliminary passes is thus the resolution of ambiguous word-class membership.

It is, furthermore, reasonable to expect that sentences will contain discontinuous fused units, that is, fused units interrupted by variously structured intervening elements. Unless such intervening structures are properly identified in prior elimination passes, the program will not be able to skip over them in the search for elements functionally relevant to the objectives of the later syntactic passes.

Finally, given the relative independence of the internal structure and the external functioning of units, alluded to further above, a number of constructions can be expected within each sentence which by their internal structure resemble potential major clause members, but do not in effect have that external functioning.

An example of this are relative clauses: their internal structure resembles that of a main clause, and they contain similarly structured clause members, but their external functioning is that of inclusion in nominal blocks as modifying elements. Constructions such as these have to be identified by appropriate preliminary passes and their boundaries and functions recorded for inclusion in the main syntax.

Once the inventory of linguistic problems has thus been systematically formulated and related to the general characteristics of the syntactic retrieval program, the actual operational sequence of passes will have to be ascertained by programming experimentation. It depends not only on the grammatical ordering of the data but also, and primarily, on the input and output features of the various passes. In addition to linguistic necessity which dictates the handling of certain information by preliminary passes, considerations of programming convenience and efficiency may lead to an increase in the number of passes, or conversely, bring about the merger of several passes into one. The pass method provides the frame within which the problems can be isolated well enough to allow control, and be viewed in a sufficiently general perspective to allow coordination and flexibility.*

* Note that this proposed syntactic retrieval algorithm has since been fully implemented as an experimental program, called the *Fulcrum I* Program, at The Bunker-Ramo Corporation, Canoga Park, California.

MACHINE TRANSLATION TODAY : THE FULCRUM APPROACH AND HEURISTICS*

1. THEORETICAL FOUNDATIONS

The theoretical conception on which the Fulcrum approach is based is the definitional model of language, In this conception, the system of a language is considered to be, not a single hierarchy with a single set of levels ascending from phonology to semantics via syntax, but a multiple hierarchy structured in two dimensions, at least one of which in turn has three planes, with a separate set of levels proper to each of the planes.[1]

Language is viewed as a system of signs structured in two dimensions, those of the grammar and the lexicon. These two dimensions differ in terms of the purpose to which the signaling means of the language are put: the lexical dimension is defined as the system of reference to culturally recognized types of phenomena; the grammatical dimension is defined as the structure of discourse.[2]

The grammatical dimension of language is characterized by three planes, each with its own set of distinctions: the plane of structuring, characterized in all languages by two *levels of structuring* — those of *phonemics* and *morphemics* (the latter including both morphology and syntax); the plane of integration, characterized in all languages by several *levels of integration* (the number

* This paper is a revised version of Progress Report No. 14 under Contract NSF-C372, "Computer-aided research in machine translation", with the National Science Foundation. The research was conducted and the paper was written while the author was at The Bunker-Ramo Corporation, Canoga Park, Calif.

1 For a detailed discussion of an earlier formulation, see Garvin 1963a. For a more recent, but more concise discussion, see Garvin 1968.

2 For a detailed discussion of the two dimensions, see Mathiot 1967.

of which varies from language to language); the plane of organization, characterized in all languages by two *organizing principles* — those of *selection* and *arrangement*.

All of these distinctions are defined by functional criteria:

1. The two levels of structuring differ in terms of the extent to which the units of each level participate in the sign function (meaning) of language. The units of the phonemic level function primarily as differentiators of the sign function, the units of the morphemic level function as its carriers.

2. The levels of integration differ in terms of the order of complexity of the units that constitute them: they range from the level of minimal units, which is the lowest, to the level of the maximal fused units, which is the highest. Fused units are considered to be not mere sequences of units of a lower order, but to function as entities of their own order, with certain overall qualities above and beyond the mere sum of their constituents.

A correlate of the concept of fused units is the conception that the internal structure and the external functioning of a given unit are separate and potentially independent characteristics: units with the same internal structure may have different external functioning; units with different internal structure may have the same external functioning.

Units with the same internal structure are called *identically constituted*; units with the same external functioning are called *functionally equivalent*.

3. The two organizing principles on the plane of organization characterize different manners in which the signaling means of the language are employed: selection from an inventory versus arrangement in a sequence.

The three planes of the grammatical dimension of language are in a hierarchical relation to each other. The plane of structuring is defined by the most significant functional criterion and is therefore superordinate to the other two planes. Of the latter, the plane of integration is in turn superordinate to the plane of organization. Consequently, within each level of the plane of structuring a set of levels of integration can be defined, and within each level of integration of either level of structuring, the operation of both organizing principles can be discerned.

This conception of the structure of natural language is only an approximation: like all natural objects, natural language exhibits many indeterminacies and is more complex than any conceptualization of it can be.

One conspicuous instance of the indeterminacies of natural languages is the perturbation of the covariance of form and meaning (which follows from the sign nature of language) by the well-known phenomena of homonymy and synonymy. Another instance is the lack of precision in the separateness of the levels of language, as shown by the presence of some aspects of meaning (rather than mere differentiation) in certain phenomena usually assigned to the phonemic level of structuring (for instance, intonation, emphatic stress).

The complexity of natural language is apparent from the observation that in its overt manifestations (text, speech behavior, etc.) the different aspects (dimensions, planes, levels) of its underlying structure are not displayed separately but are closely intertwined, in the sense that each individual manifestation of the system displays all of its aspects together in a complex signal.

It is because of these indeterminacies and complexities that the model chosen for the conceptual representation of natural language is not quantitative, but qualitative. The model postulates only the general attributes of the object of study, but not the specific values and detailed manifestations of these attributes. These are to be ascertained by empirical means. Thus, the statement of the structure of a particular language is not considered a theory of this language, but rather a description within the frame of reference provided by a theory.[3]

In a linguistic description based on the definitional model, the various features of the model determine the organization of the description as follows:

[3] The classical statement of the opposite view is found in Chomsky 1957: 49: "A grammar of the language L is essentially a theory of L".

1. The concept of the separateness of the two dimensions of language provides the justification for limiting the description to either of the two dimensions, and for keeping the grammar separate from the lexicon;

2. The concept of the levels of phonemics and morphemics on the plane of structuring provides the reason for differentiating the description of the phonemic pattern from that of the morphemic pattern, and to deal with their interrelations as a distinct aspect of the description;

3. The concept of the levels of integration provides the reason for organizing the description in terms of both minimal units and various orders of fused units, on both the phonemic and morphemic levels of structuring;

4. The concept of the potential independence of internal structure and external functioning provides the reason for differentiating these two aspects of linguistic units throughout the description;

5. The concept of the organizing principles of selection and arrangement on the plane of organization provides the reason for including in the description not only the inventories of units but also their distribution.

In the development of the Fulcrum approach, the primary concentration has not been on the further elaboration of the theoretical model of language, but on the design of a system appropriate to the task of translation, as well as the conduct of appropriate experimentation to test the adequacy of the system to the task. In the design of this system, the various features of the definitional model of language have served as guidelines but, by contrast with some other approaches to language data processing, the Fulcrum system is not intended to be a direct computer implementation of the underlying model. Rather, the function of the model is, from an operational point of view, to serve as a frame of reference for the design of the system, and from a theoretical point of view, to provide an explication and justification for the system.[4]

[4] For a different conception of the role of the model in a machine translation system, see Lamb 1965.

In this connection, it is important to note a basic difference between the application of the definitional model to linguistic description, and its application to the design of a machine translation system.

As was noted from the above, the organization of a linguistic description closely follows the hierarchic structure of the model. This is because, on the one hand, the model is considered a conceptual representation of the phenomenon of natural language in terms of its general properties, and on the other hand, a linguistic description presents the specific manifestation of these general properties in the case of a particular language.

In the design of the Fulcrum system, on the other hand, the properties of language as stipulated by the definitional model are taken into account in the order in which they are relevant to the process of translation. This order does not coincide with their organization within the model and the linguistic description.

Thus, the plane of organization, which ranks low in the hierarchy of planes of the grammatical dimension, is of primary significance in the theoretical interpretation of the translation process. The two organizing principles of selection and arrangement have been identified as the two basic components of the translation process since the early days of machine translation research (see pp. 66-72).

Of at least equal importance is the plane of integration. The syntactic recognition routines of the translation algorithm are formulated in terms of the requirement of identifying the boundaries and functions of syntactic fused units (Garvin, 1963b, see also p. 83).

The plane of structuring applies to machine translation in the relatively obvious sense that the machine-readable input symbols (letters, spaces, etc.) belong to the graphemic level (which is functionally equivalent to the phonemic level of spoken language), while the units manipulated by the translation algorithm belong to the morphemic level (primarily words and syntactic fused units). The conversion from graphemic to morphemic units is accomplished by the dictionary lookup and by those subroutines of the translation algorithm which assign grammar codes (and with them morphemic status) to graphic elements not contained in the dictionary (such as symbols, missing words, etc.).

The two dimensions of language, which are kept separate in linguistic description, are taken into account together in the Fulcrum algorithm. The dictionary lookup is supplemented by special subroutines (such as the idiom and word combination routines) which allow the processing as single translation units of not only individual words, but also multiword lexical units. The syntactic recognition routines then treat these lexical units in the same way as syntactic units of similar structure that have been identified on the basis of purely grammatical criteria.

2. GENERAL CHARACTERISTICS OF THE FULCRUM APPROACH

The Fulcrum approach differs from other approaches for automatic sentence structure determination primarily in the following respects:

1. The Fulcrum approach favors a bipartite, rather than a tripartite, organization of the parsing system.
2. The Fulcrum approach is characterized by two basic operational principles: (a) the concept of the fulcrum; (b) the pass method.
3. The Fulcrum approach aims at producing a single interpretation of each individual sentence, rather than at producing all conceivable interpretations.

Each of these characteristics will now be discussed further.

2.1. *Bipartite organization*

A bipartite parsing system consists of two basic components: a dictionary with grammar codes (and other codes), and an algorithm which contains both the processing subroutines and the information required for processing. A tripartite parsing system consists of three basic components: a dictionary with grammar codes (and other codes), a processing algorithm, and a separate store of information (such as a table of grammar rules and other rule tables) which is called by the algorithm. The basic difference between these two types of system thus is that in a bipartite system the information required by the algorithm is written right into it, while in a tripartite system processor and information are kept separate.

Two types of advantages of the tripartite approach are usually cited by its proponents:

1. It separates the labor of the programmer who designs and maintains the processor from that of the linguist who designs and maintains the table of rules. The only thing they have to agree on is the format of the rules that the processor can accept. This minimizes the communication problem between linguist and programmer, since once these matters have been settled, the two portions of the program can be handled separately.

2. The same processor can be used with more than one table of rules. This means first of all that rules can be modified or changed without having to change the processor, provided of course that the format is maintained. This gives the linguist great freedom of experimentation with different types of rules. It also permits the use of the same processor for the parsing of more than one language, by simply substituting one table of rules for another.

These advantages apply particularly well to small experimental systems oriented towards linguistic research; for larger-scale experimentation, oriented towards the processing of randomly chosen bodies of text with the ultimate aim of designing an operational translation system, the advantages of a tripartite system are less clearcut. This is why the Fulctum approach favors a bipartite organization of the parsing system.[5]

The algorithm of a bipartite system is essentially not a 'parser' of the type used in tripartite systems. It is instead a linguistic pattern recognition algorithm which, instead of matching portions of sentences against rules stored in a table, directs searches at the different portions of the sentence in order to identify its grammatical and lexical pattern. Thus, the essential characteristic of the

[5] For a more detailed discussion of the reasons for this preference, see pp. 43-47.

algorithm is the sequencing of the searches, and in each search subroutine, only as much grammatical and lexical information is used as is appropriate to the particular search. The rules of the grammar and lexicon are in fact applied by the algorithm in a definite order, and a given rule is not even called unless the previous searches have led to a point where its application becomes necessary. This means that the highly complex system of rules that makes up the real grammar and lexicon of a language is distributed over a correspondingly complex algorithm which applies the rules in terms of the ordering that the structure of the language requires.

The description of Russian which furnishes the information included in the Fulcrum algorithm is based on the definitional model of language. It was developed using conventional Russian grammars and dictionaries as a starting point, verifying the reliability of the information, and adapting it to the requirements of the Fulcrum approach. In this process, it was found that many of the conventionally accepted statements about Russian grammar are not only inaccurate, but also that they are insufficient for purposes of automatic syntactic recognition. This is particularly true with respect to government, complementation, and mandatory co-occurrence relations.

2.2. *Fulcra and passes*

A bipartite system stands or falls by the manner in which the problem of the sequencing of the searches within the algorithm has been solved. This is the key problem in developing the detailed structure of the algorithm.

The Fulcrum approach attempts to solve this problem by using two fundamental principles: the concept of the fulcrum and the pass method.

The concept of the fulcrum implies the use of key elements within the sentence (fulcra) as starting points for the searches performed by the algorithm. This means that the algorithm, in searching through a sentence, does not simply progress from word to word, but in fact 'skips' from fulcrum to fulcrum. It performs a little search sequence each time it has reached a fulcrum, and goes on to the next fulcrum when this particular search is completed.

The pass method means that not one, but several passes are made at every sentence, each pass designed to identify a particular set of grammatical conditions pertinent to the recognition process. Consequently, each pass has its own set of fulcra and its own search sequences. The pass method reflects the orderly progression in which the determination of the structure of the sentence is made: first, the sentence components are identified individually, then the relations between components are established, and finally the structure of the sentence as a whole is established. To each of these intermediate parsing objectives there corresponds, roughly, a pass or series of passes in the algorithm. The correspondence is not exact, because there are many ambiguities and irregularities interfering with the recognition process, and the design of the Fulcrum algorithm reflects these added complexities.

2.3. *Single interpretation of each sentence*

Many automatic parsing systems are theory-oriented: their aim is to apply, verify, or otherwise deal with, a formal model of language, such as, for instance, a particular variety of phrase-structure grammars. One of the significant theoretical results of the use of such a parsing system is the determination of all the conceivable parsings that a given sentence is assigned by a particular grammar.[6]

The Fulcrum approach, on the other hand, is translation-oriented. Its aim is primarily to produce as correct a translation as possible. Clearly, for this purpose, the identification of all conceivable parsings of a given sentence is of no great interest. Rather, it is desirable for the algorithm to produce, at all times, if not the correct parsing, at least the most likely parsing of each sentence, to serve as the basis for its translation from Russian into English. In the earlier versions of the Fulcrum approach, this unique par-

[6] Cf. Kuno 1965: 453: "A predictive analyzer produces for a given sentence all possible syntactic interpretations compatible with the current version of the predictive grammar".

sing was chosen deterministically on the basis of the contextual information available to it: for each set of conditions as identified by previous and current searches, the single possible — or most probable — interpretation was assigned to each syntactic and lexical configuration.

Thus, Russian clauses in which a nominal structure, ambiguously either nominative or accusative, both precedes and follows a predicate that agrees with either nominal structure, were interpreted by the algorithm on the basis of the highest probability in syntactic terms: the structure to the left of the predicate was interpreted as subject, that to the right of the predicate as object. The alternative interpretation (object-predicate-subject), although theoretically conceivable, was ignored. In the overwhelming majority of instances of course, this turns out to be the correct interpretation, as shown by the Russian one-clause sentence: Это предложение сохраняет нормальный порядок which has only one reasonable interpretation: 'This sentence preserves normal order'.

There are a few structural configurations in which this probabilistic interpretation is not necessarily (or not at all) the correct one. First of all, there are some Russian clauses which, when used out of context, have only the one reasonable interpretation of consisting of subject-predicate-object. But, because of their particular lexical structure, they require the alternative interpretation in certain contexts. So, for instance, the Russian one-clause sentence Автобусы заменили тролейбусы. would ordinarily be interpreted as: 'Motor buses have replaced trolleybuses'. But not so in the special context in which this sentence is preceded by У нас уже нет автобусов 'We no longer have motor buses'.[7] This context requires the alternative interpretation of object-predicate-subject: 'Trolleybuses have replaced motor buses'. (A stylistically better English translation would preserve order and replace the active predicate by a passive: 'Motor buses have been replaced by trolleybuses'.) There are, finally, a few Russian clauses which in any context have only the alternative interpretation (object-predicate-subject).

[7] I am indebted to A. Isačenko for this example.

The classical example of these constructions is Большой интерес представляет вопрос... which, because of its particular lexical structure, can only be interpreted as object-predicate-subject: 'Of great interest is the question...'.

The principle followed here is that, as the searching capability of the algorithm increases, the likelihood of erroneous choices decreases correspondingly. Thus, by increasing the lexical recognition capability of the algorithm, constructions of the last-mentioned type, in which lexical conditions override the effect of the syntactic configuration, can be identified and translated correctly. By increasing the range of contexts that the algorithm can search, constructions of the first-mentioned type, in which contextual factors override the effect of the syntactic configuration, can be identified and translated correctly. Clearly, the former recognition problem is much easier to resolve than the latter, since it requires only that special lexical meanings be taken into account, while the latter requires a form of 'understanding' by the algorithm of the specific content of individual sentences.

Problems of the type just discussed are still within the capabilities of a deterministic recognition algorithm. There are, however, a number of identification problems of a different type which transcend the scope of a deterministic resolution capability and which require a heuristic approach to syntactic recognition. These will be discussed in sections 3 and thereafther.

2.4. *Current status*

The Fulcrum syntactic analyzer has been implemented on two levels: (a) an earlier, less sophisticated version called *Fulcrum I* (see pp. 83-89), which was fully coded and is now capable of producing experimental translations; (b) a recent more sophisticated version, called *Fulcrum II,* for which detailed plans were drawn up and which, when implemented on a general-purpose computer, will be capable of producing translations for practical use. It is expected that the complete implementation of the Fulcrum II, given appropriate funding and staffing, might take four to six years.

The major improvements in the *Fulcrum II* over *Fulcrum I* are the following:

a. The order of passes and individual search operations deviates further from the order of descriptive levels than was the case in *Fulcrum I.* This is due to the fact that the new search patterns are based primarily on the order in which the grammatical information becomes available to the program rather than the order in which a linguist would prefer to present his description.

b. The *Fulcrum II* uses an iterative principle. The same set of search operations is used repeatedly to establish the internal structure of a variety of syntactic units. Thus, inserted structures (such as parenthetic expressions) are treated by the same search operation as entire sentences; clauses of different types, such as relative clauses or independent clauses, are likewise treated by essentially the same search sequence. A control cycle insures that the different search sequences are called in the right order so that these different units are identified and related to each other appropriately.

c. The heuristic principle of trial and evaluation (see below) is applied throughout the *Fulcrum II* algorithm. In all parts in the program where decisions are not unequivocal, a capability will exist for labeling decisions as provisional trials, so that they can be revised later in the program by evaluation routines based on information available to the program subsequently.

3. THE NEED FOR HEURISTICS

The problems of the types treated in the preceding sections do not require a revision of the basic design of the earlier versions of the Fulcrum algorithm. They do require access to more information of more kinds, but within the framework of the original pass method — perhaps with an increased number of passes, or an improved overall layout of passes.

There are, however, a number of recognition problems for which the original deterministic design is inherently inadequate. These are the cases in which the correct resolution of a problem arising in a given pass requires the use of information that only a later pass can provide. From the standpoint of syntactic and lexical configuration, these are the instances in which the immediate context suggests the probability of a certain identification which, however, in the light of the total context of the sentence turns out to be incorrect.

The classical example of this type of configuration is the genitive singular/nominative-accusative plural ambiguity of nominals, the resolution of which as a genitive is suggested by an immediately preceding nominal structure. This identification, though correct in the majority of examples in Russian technical text, may turn out to be erroneous if other conditions in the broader context prevail; for instance, if a plural subject is required for the predicate of the clause and only the ambiguous nominal is an available candidate. This configuration is shown by the nominal задачи 'of a task/tasks' in the clause В нашем плане задачи будут выполнеы 'In our plan, the tasks will be fulfilled...' Note that the resolution based on the immediate context is still likely to be the correct one in the majority of instances; it is the 'usual' resolution which should be overridden only under 'special' conditions.

One treatment of the type of problem illustrated by the above example would be for the algorithm to record both possible interpretations of the ambiguous form early in the program, and make the selection later when the information from the broader context has also become available. This resolution would, however, fail to take into account the characteristic feature of this type of configuration, which is that the two possible resolutions of the syntactic ambiguity are not equally probable: in the majority of occurrences, a correct identification can be based on the immediate context, and the broader context has to be resorted to only under special conditions. This requires a method of resolution which will accept an identification based on the immediate context, will let it stand in the majority of cases, but will have the capability for revising this decision in all those cases in which the special conditions apply which call for an identification in terms of the broader context. Such a method of resolution is heuristic in nature; it is discussed in detail in the subsequent sections.

4. HEURISTIC PRINCIPLES

The Fulcrum approach has borrowed the concept of heuristics from its applications in artificial intelligence research.

As is well known, the concept of heuristics is related to problem-solving. This is how most students of artificial intelligence speak of it. According to M. Minsky (Feigenbaum and Feldman, 1963: 407), "The adjective 'heuristic', as used here and widely in the literature, means *related to improving problem-solving performance*; as a noun, it is also used in regard to any method or trick used to improve the efficiency of a problem-solving system". G. Pask (1964: 168) speaks of "... a set of 'heuristics' ... or broad rules and suggestions for problem solution ...".

One characteristic of heuristics is that it is "provisional and plausible" (H. Gelernter in Feigenbaum and Feldman, 1963: 135). Another more important characteristic is that they are "processes ... which generally contribute to a result but whose effects are not 'guaranteed' " (Newell and Simon, 1963: 390).

The major advantage of heuristic principles is considered to be that they "contribute, on the average, to reduction of search in problem-solving activity". (F. M. Tonge in Feigenbaum and Feldman, 1963: 172). Thus, "... a heuristic procedure substitutes the effort reduction of its shortcuts for the guaranteed optimal solution of an exhaustive method ..." (ibid., 173).

Theorists of heuristics often speak of heuristic processes. The mathematician G. Polya, who is often cited as an authority on heuristics by students of artificial intelligence, defines modern heuristics as the study of "the process of solving problems" (1957: 129). He links the use of heuristics to plausible reasoning, as applied in the "heuristic syllogism", which he differentiates from the demonstrative reasoning of logic (ibid. 186-190). Others emphasize the methodological aspects of heuristics. Thus, E. A. Guillemin (1931: 10) speaks of "... a method of solution ... which is used almost exclusively by physicists and engineers. This method is nothing more than judicious guessing. The elegant title by which this method is known is the *heuristic method*".

All of the above-noted aspects of heuristics have to do with the general functional characteristics of heuristic processes or methods. Clearly, they all are in some way pertinent to syntactic resolution in general and the Fulcrum approach in particular. We are dealing with a form of problem-solving; the solutions may have to be provisional and plausible rather than definitive, and they are certainly not guaranteed; the Fulcrum approach, at least, has as one of its major aims the reduction of the number of required searches; certainly, all forms of syntactic resolution are based on plausible rather than demonstrative reasoning, and are in essence well-organized judicious guesses.

In view of all this, it might not be unreasonable to refer to all syntactic recognition procedures as recognition heuristics. The reason this has not been done is because in the Fulcrum approach a somewhat more specific and restricted definition of heuristics has been used than that implicit in the aspects listed so far.

Such a more specific definition is based on the design characteristics of a heuristic program, rather than on the general purpose of the heuristic approach. While these design characteristics are not explicitly stated in the literature, they can be extrapolated from an examination of the use of heuristics in artificial intelligence (cf. several of the articles in Feigenbaum and Feldman, 1963). In essence, a heuristic program consists of an alternation of trials and evaluations based on a clearly defined strategy. The strategy is that of a problem-solver, the trials are the "judicious guesses" (see above) which characterize the heuristic method, and the evaluation of the trials is based on criteria of goal attainment derived from a definition of the problem.[8]

[8] For a more detailed discussion of this view of heuristics, see Garvin 1964: 80-85.

Usually a heuristic program and an algorithm are considered two alternative ways of approaching a problem. Thus, A. Newell, J. C. Shaw, and H. A. Simon note (Feigenbaum and Feldman, 1963: 114) that there may be "both algorithms and heuristics as alternatives for solving the same problem". In the Fulcrum approach, on the other hand, heuristics is not used as an alternative to an algorithm. Rather, the two are combined in the same program: the Fulcrum algorithm contains certain heuristic portions designed for the resolution of only those identification problems that do not lend themselves to a straightforward algorithmic treatment. This means that the Fulcrum algorithm, in addition to the heuristic trial and evaluation components, must also contain provisions for identifying those sets of conditions under which heuristic resolution is required.

These design features of the heuristic portions of the Fulcrum algorithm will be discussed in the subsequent section.

5. DESIGN OF THE HEURISTIC PORTIONS OF THE FULCRUM ALGORITHM

As has been noted in the preceding section, the design of the heuristic aspects of the Fulcrum algorithm is not identical with that of an independent heuristic program. Rather, the need to adapt the heuristic design principles to the requirements of the Fulcrum approach has led to the development of a design quite specific to this particular purpose.

The most typical feature of this design has already been mentioned, namely, the overall characteristic that the heuristic is, as it were, embedded in an algorithm. Thus, the executive routine of the heuristic, which carries out the 'guessing' strategy by calling the trial and evaluation routines, in fact constitutes a bridge between the deterministic main portion of the algorithm and the heuristic portion. It operates on the basis of a capability of the deterministic main portion of the algorithm for recognizing when to call the heuristic portion. This capability is one for recognizing the circumstance, already noted previously, that for a given ambiguously interpretable form the conditions present in the immediate context do not guarantee a correct identification. Once this recognition has been effected, the Fulcrum algorithm makes the transition from the deterministic main portion to the heuristic portion and acts as the executive routine of the heuristic.

The remaining aspects of the heuristic portion of the Fulcrum algorithm, namely, those dealing with the conduct of the trials and evaluations, likewise differ significantly in their design from an independent heuristic program.

An independent heuristic program, such as those used for game-playing or theorem-proving (see Feigenbaum and Feldman, 1963), carries out more than one trial every time it 'considers' a particular move or other operation. By contrast, the heuristic portion of the Fulcrum algorithm conducts only one trial each time it is called, or more specifically, it carries out a particular single syntactic identification in the form of a trial, subject to later revision. The question asked in an independent heuristic thus is, which of several trials (if any) is successful? The question asked by the heuristic portion of the Fulcrum algorithm is, is this particular trial successful?

In an independent heuristic, evaluation takes place immediately after each given set of trials has been completed. In the heuristic portion of the Fulcrum algorithm, the evaluation of a given trial identification does not take place until later in the program. This is because, as was repeatedly noted before, the trial identification is based on the broader context, and the Fulcrum algorithm deals with the immediate context significantly earlier in the program than with the broader context.

As in any heuristic, so in the heuristic portion of the Fulcrum algorithm, the essential subject-matter question concerns the factors on which the trials and evaluations are based.

In the heuristic syntax, the trials are based on probability: as has already been noted, a given trial identification is always made on the basis of the most likely solution suggested by the immediate context. It must be stressed that this likelihood is determined impressionistically on the basis of available knowledge of Russian grammar; it is not considered necessary to have recourse to a formal probability calculus. The evaluations are based primarily on the mandatoriness of certain syntactic relations within the broader context: if the broader context requires that a certain syntactic function (such as that of subject) be filled, and this condition can be met only by revising a previous trial identification, then this requirement constitutes the evaluation criterion on the basis of which the original trial is rejected and an alternative solution is substituted for it.

The heuristic portion of the Fulcrum algorithm operates in the following manner. Whenever the recognition routines identify a set of conditions under which a trial identification is made, a record of this trial is written (a heuristic 'flag' is 'set'). When later in the program the broader context requires a mandatory syntactic component for which no suitable candidate is present, the algorithm 'looks for' a heuristic flag. If it finds a flag, the trial identification is judged a failure on the basis of the newly encountered conditions of mandatoriness, and the alternative identification is chosen in its stead, in order to satisfy this condition of mandatoriness.

As can be inferred from the above, the use of heuristics in syntax presupposes the inclusion in the grammar code of the Fulcrum system of all those indications that are essential to the operation of the heuristic portion of the algorithm. In particular, this means including information about mandatoriness of syntactic relations where this is not implicit in the word class of the dictionary entry. Thus, for every attributive (adjective or adjectival pronoun), a head is mandatory and hence no special mandatoriness notation is required in the grammar code. In the case of predicatives, on the other hand, a subject or object may be either optional or mandatory, and hence a mandatoriness notation in the grammar code is necessary.

Specific examples of heuristic ambiguity resolution in the Fulcrum algorithm are discussed in the subsequent section.

6. APPLICATION OF HEURISTICS TO PARTICULAR SYNTACTIC RESOLUTION PROBLEMS

Two areas of syntactic resolution will be discussed to illustrate the application of the heuristic portion of the Fulcrum algorithm. These are the syntactic interpretation of genitive nominal blocks and the resolution of predicative-adverb homographs (word-class ambiguities of the type ясно). Genitive nominal blocks here include both those that are unambiguously genitives and those that are ambiguously genitives. The latter are nominal blocks which in addition to the genitive function have other case functions, requiring the resolution of the case ambiguity in addition to other aspects of syntactic identification.

6.1. *Genitive nominal blocks*

The cases of interest here are those for which the immediate context suggests that the (unambiguously or ambiguously) genitive block functions as an adnominal genitive complement. This resolution may be overridden by conditions in the broader context which the heuristic capability of the program recognizes.

Thus, the ambiguous genitive полета '(of) flight' in the immediate context время полета 'time (of) flight' will be identified as the adnominal genitive complement. However, the broader context may require that this genitive form be interpreted as the genitive of reference of a negative predicate, as when the above example is expanded to read: В это время полета не было 'at this time there was no flight'. The heuristic capability of the program will then carry out the required revision of identification.

Other types of conditions in the broader context which may require heuristic revision are:

1. Genitive nominal block is required as head of a (governing) modifier;
2. Genitive nominal block is required as subject of a predicate;
3. Genitive nominal block is needed as object of predicate;
4. Genitive nominal block is required as genitive of subject or object of deverbative noun.

Note than in each of the above cases, a relation in the broader context (head of modifier, subject of clause, etc.) is considered mandatory. In order to comply with this condition of mandatoriness, the previous identification based on the immediate context is overridden, and an identification which satisfies the mandatory relation in the broader context is substituted.

The types of conditions listed above are illustrated by the following examples.

(1) Выполненные бригадой работы...

The immediate context here suggests the trial identification of the ambiguously genitive noun работы '(of) work(s)' as the adnominal genitive complement to бригадой '(by) the brigade', to read бригадой работы '(by) the work brigade'. The broader context, however, requires that a head be assigned to the nominative/accusative plural governing modifier (past passive participle) выполненные 'performed', and the ambiguously genitive noun работы (which can also function as nominative/accusative plural) is the only available candidate. Consequently, the trial identification as genitive adnominal complement is rejected, and replaced by a definitive identification as head to the governing modifier. The sentence fragment is then interpreted correctly as reading 'work performed by the brigade'.

(2) В эксперименте цели будут выполнены...

The immediate context here again suggests the trial identification of the ambiguously genitive noun цели '(of/to/by) goal(s)' as the adnominal genitive complement to эксперименте 'experiment'. The broader context, however, requires that a subject be assigned to the plural predicate будут выполнены 'will be fulfilled', and the ambiguously genitive noun цели (which can also function as nominative/accusative plural) is the only available candidate. Consequently, the trial identification as adnominal genitive complement is rejected and replaced by the definitive identification as subject. The sentence fragment is then interpreted correctly as reading 'In the experiment the goals will be fulfilled ...'

(3) Данный метод результата не дает.

The immediate context suggests the trial identification of the unambiguously genitive noun результата '(of) result' as the adnominal genitive complement to данный метод '(the) given method'. The broader context, however, requires that an object in the genitive be assigned to the negative predicate не дает 'does not give', and the unambiguously genitive noun результата is the only available candidate. Consequently, the trial identification as adnominal genitive complement is rejected and replaced by a definitive identification as object. The sentence is then interpreted correctly as 'The given method gives no result'.

(4) определение с максимальной точностью формы диаграммы

Again, the immediate context suggests the trial identification of the ambiguously genitive noun формы '(of) form(s)' as the adnominal genitive complement to точностью '(by) accuracy'. However, the broader context requires that a genitive of object be assigned to the deverbative noun определение 'determination', and the ambiguously genitive noun формы is the only a available candidate. Consequently, the trial identification is rejected and replaced by a definitive identification as genitive of object. The sentence fragment is then interpreted correctly as reading 'The determination of the form of the diagram with maximum accuracy'.

6.2. *Predicative-adverb homographs*

The cases of interest here are those for which the immediate context suggests that the homograph functions as an adverb. This resolution may be overridden by mandatory conditions in the broader context which the heuristic capability of the program recognizes.

Thus, the homograph понятно 'is understandable/understandably' will be identified as an adverb in the immediate context понятно высказанное 'understandably voiced'. However, the broader context may require that this homograph be interpreted a a predicative, as when the above example is expanded to read: Нам понятно высказанное И. П. Павловым убеждение. что... 'We understand the conviction voiced by I. P. Pavlov, that ... (lit.: the conviction ... is understandable to us)'. The heuristic capability of the program will then carry out the required revision of identification.

The mandatory condition in the broader context here is, of course, that a clause should have a predicate whenever any candidate at all is available. Since the neuter nominative nominal block высказанное И. П. Павловым убеждение qualifies as subject, and the nominal block нам qualifies as the appropriate dative object, the homograph reinterpreted as a neuter predicative will meet both the condition of agreeing with the subject and the condition of governing the object, thus providing the clause with the needed predicate.

7. IMPLEMENTATION OF HEURISTIC SYNTAX

The essential characteristics of heuristic syntax as applied in the Fulcrum approach can be summed up as follows:

1. The heuristic portion of the Fulcrum algorithm is called whenever there is a possibility that a given identification made on the basis of the immediate context may have to be revised on the basis of information provided by the broader context.
2. The conditions requiring the use of heuristics are recognized by the deterministic portion of the Fulcrum algorithm.
3. The mechanism for calling the heuristic syntax consists in the writing of a record (setting a 'flag') in the sentence image which the program produces, indicating that a given identification has been made on a trial basis and is subject to heuristic revision.

4. The evaluation criteria for the revision of trial identifications consist in various conditions of mandatoriness of occurrence of certain syntactic components. These conditions are recorded in the grammar codes of the dictionary entries which the Fulcrum algorithm manipulates. Some of these conditions are contained in the grammar codes by implication: thus, the word class code notation 'modifier' implies the requirement of a head to which this modifier is to be assigned. Other conditions must be noted explicitly in the grammar code, for instance, the mandatoriness of subjects or objects for certain predicatives, or the mandatoriness of genitives of subject or object for certain deverbative nouns.

5. The mechanism for applying a heuristic revision to a trial identification consists of the following:

(a) The program first notes the absence of a mandatory syntactic element by acting upon the requirements implicit in the grammar code, or by reading the specific mandatoriness notation.

(b) The program now tests for the presence of heuristic decision records ('flags') in the sentence image and checks whether the recorded element is a suitable candidate for the missing syntactic component.

(c) If these tests are positive, the trial identification is revised and a definitive identification is substituted for it.

As can be noted, the apparatus for the heuristic syntax consists primarily of a capability for recognizing the need for heuristics, suitable notations in the grammar code to allow the heuristic evaluation of trial identifications, and a mechanism for writing and reading heuristic records in the sentence image, on the basis of which the revision of trial identifications can take place.

REFERENCES

Chomsky, N.
1957 *Syntactic Structures* (The Hague, Mouton).
Feigenbaum, E. A. and J. Feldman, eds.
1963 *Computers and Thought* (New York, McGraw-Hill).

Garvin, P. L.
1963a "The definitional model of language", *Natural Language and the Computer*, ed. by Paul L. Garvin (New York, McGraw-Hill), pp. 3-22.
1963b "Syntax in machine translation", *Natural Language and the Computer*, ed. by Paul L. Garvin (New York, McGraw-Hill), pp. 223-32.
1964 "Automatic linguistic analysis — A heuristic problem", *On Linguistic Method* (The Hague, Mouton), pp. 78-97.
1967 "The Fulcrum syntactic analyzer for Russian", *preprints for 2ème Conférence Internationale sur le Traitement Automatique des Langues. Grenoble, 23-25 août 1967*. Paper No. 5.
1968 "The role of function in linguistic theory", *Proc. of the X Internat. Congress of Linguists, Bucharest, 1967*, vol. I, pp. 287-91.
Guillemin, E. A.
1931 *Communication Networks*, Vol. 1 (New York, Wiley).
Kuno, S.
1965 "The predictive analyzer and a path elimination technique", *Communications of the ACM* 8.453-62. Reprinted in David G. Hays, *Readings in Automatic Language Processing* (New York, American Elsevier, 1966), pp. 83-106.
Lamb, S. M.
1965 "The nature of the machine translation problem", *Journal of Verbal Learning and Verbal Behavior* 4. 196-211.
Mathiot, M.
1967 "The place of the dictionary in linguistic description", *Language* 43. 703-24.
Newell, A. and H. A. Simon
1963 "Computers in psychology", *Handbook of Mathematical Psychology*, ed. by R. Duncan Luce, Robert R. Bush, Eugene Galanter. Vol. 1 (New York, Wiley), pp. 361-428.
Pask, G.
1964 "A discussion of artificial intelligence and self-organization", *Advances in Computers*, ed. by Franz L. Alt and Morris Rubinoff. Vol. 5 (New York and London, Academic Press), pp. 109-226.
Polya, G.
1957 *How to Solve it* (Garden City. N. Y., Doubleday).

IV

IMPLICATIONS

DEGREES OF COMPUTER PARTICIPATION IN LINGUISTIC RESEARCH*

1. This paper is not designed as a survey of the field of language data processing. My views on this are set forth in some detail elsewhere.[1] Rather, the purpose of this paper is to consider the varying extent to which a computer program can be integrated into the process of linguistic research itself. I am here limiting myself to descriptive linguistics.

It is no longer necessary to point out that computers are capable of the very rapid processing of extremely large bodies of data. Not is it necessary to labor the point that the quality of computer application is no better than the research design devised by the user. While in essence computer operations consist of nothing but a series of extremely elementary instructions strung together in a program, the variety of tasks for which this programming string can be used is considerable.

From a linguist's standpoint, computer applications can be considered in terms of the degree to which they form part of the process of the research itself: from applications that merely simplify or make possible the book-keeping of copious research data, to applications in which the program is based on structural information or analytic rules.

At present three such degrees of computer participation can be set forth: language data collection, which is essentially a form of

* Work on this paper was done at Thompson-Rame-Wooldridge, Inc., under the sponsorship of the Office of Scientific Research of the Office of Aerospace Research under Contract No. AF 49(638)-1128. It was prepared for presentation at the Burg Wartenstein symposium No. 18 of the Wenner-Gren Foundation for Anthropological Research: The Use of Computers in Anthropology, 20-30 June, 1962.

[1] See pp. 15-39:

bookkeeping; computer programs using the results of linguistic research; and automation of linguistic research procedures.

2. The purpose of language data collection is to collect linguistic data in a systematic way in order to make them available for convenient inspection by the researcher. The most common form of this is the compilation of concordances. Without extensive syntactic processing of the text, concordances are limited to the inclusion, together with the word of interest, of a specified number of additional words to the left or right in the immediate neighborhood, or of all the words reaching in both directions from the given word to a particular punctuation mark. The usefulness of concordances is unquestioned, but from the researcher's standpoint they constitute no more than an organized file of raw data.

A form of language data collection which does more data processing for the linguistic researcher than a concordance is the automatic compilation of dictionaries from texts with interlinear translation. This is a computer application which to my knowledge has not yet been tried, but which it would be relatively simple to implement from a programming standpoint. It consists in effect of not much else than the alphabetizing of every form of the original text together with the interlinear translation that goes with it. Assuming that the original has been consistently transcribed, there will now be an alphabetic file of the words of the text, and the researcher will be limited to essentially two tasks: (1) to decide how many of the alphabetized words will be part of the same lexical unit and therefore included in the same dictionary entry, and what is to be chosen as the canonical form of the entry word; and (2) to rework the interlinear translations into dictionary definitions. It is clear that this is merely the beginning of lexicographic work, if more than a simple word list is intended. For more extensive lexicographic efforts, it might be possible to combine the program suggested above with a concordance program where the researcher can use the output to expand his dictionary entries by the information contained in the concordance.

It is important in this connection to consider what are the prerequisites for such a computer application. To be possible at all, language data collection requires a text segmented into words or other units equivalent to words. This means in effect that the automatic processing of (say) medieval manuscripts without indication of word boundaries presupposes at least enough pre-editing to insert word boundaries and punctuation. Needless to say, the processing of text recorded from nonliterate languages has to meet the same requirements. In addition, the problem of consistency arises with utmost severity in both cases.

3. The most important computer application drawing upon the results of linguistic research is linguistic information processing. This is here defined to include all processing of natural language data for the purpose of extracting information from text; it includes both machine translation and information retrieval. In the present context, machine translation can be discussed with a higher degree of definiteness, since both the use of linguistic skill in machine translation research and the importance of structural information in the machine translation process are more definitely known. The present remarks will therefore be limited to machine translation, although it is assumed that as linguistic experience with information retrieval progresses, some analogous statements about the latter field may also become possible.

In machine translation it is now generally accepted that a simple dictionary lookup program, no matter how large the dictionary, just will not do. All researchers agree that a computer program for the detection of syntactic relations and semantic ambiguities is a necessary part of the machine translation process. From the standpoint of linguistic research this means in effect that the machine translation program must include, though with a special bias towards the production of a translation, a description of the source language which will allow the program to assign each portion of the text to its appropriate place in the structure. Thus, for the linguistic analyst the machine translation program is in part a special variant of the grammar of the language converted into a computer program. If indeed the computer program contains the grammar of a language, then the success of this program in effecting a translation is among other things a measure of the degree to which the grammar underlying the program correctly identifies the structure of the text in the source language: at least in machine translation it can be said that the computer program allows us to verify a linguistic description.

This is of great significance to the field of linguistic research, since experimental verification of results is usually extremely difficult in a behavioral science. In this particular case, the computer yields results which are subject to objective scrutiny, even though criteria for the quality of a translation are difficult to formulate. On the other hand, inspection by a linguist is often sufficient to ascertain whether the grammatical structure of the source text has been adequately recognized by the computer program, even where the final translation product may be deficient in other respects.

A computer application in which verification of a linguistic description constitutes not merely a by-product but, in my opinion, the major operational purpose of the program, is machine sentence generation. This is the formulation of a computer program designed to generate random sentences of a language, using a machine dictionary and a program embodying a set of co-occurrence rules. I am familiar with two approaches to machine sentence generation: one is Victor Yngve's; the other is the Auto-Beatnik project of Librascope, a division of General Precision, Inc., the linguistic aspects of which are due to R. M. Worthy.[2] The Auto-Beatnik program differs from Yngve's not only in that it is based not on a formal but on a common-sense approach to grammar, but also in that it attempts to set forth co-occurrence rules that go beyond syntax and produce 'poetry'. Both programs generate approximations of English sentences. The more closely the output approximates normal, 'grammatical' English, the more it may be assumed that the co-occurrence rules included in the program reflect the genuine conditions of the distribution of English printed

[2] Many more such programs have been devised since this paper was originally written.

words. The comparison of the output with ordinary English is done by inspection.

Of comparable significance are certain experiments in information retrieval, as exemplified by those conducted by D. R. Swanson in the early Sixties.[3] These experiments are designed to test the efficiency with which a set of technical subject-matter questions can be answered by a computer on the basis of a small library stored in memory. One of the organizing principles employed in these experiments is the use of a thesaurus in which words and phrases with common subject-matter references are grouped together. From a linguistic standpoint the major interest of this procedure is to verify the degree to which the assumed semantic similarities that have led to the compilation of the thesaurus are indeed borne out by the results of the experiment. It thus constitutes the beginnings of an experimental verification of our insights into semantic structure. The output of the program consists of a listing of documents relevant to a given request. The relevance weights of the documents retrieved by the program are automatically compared to a 'perfect retrieval score' stored in memory. In spite of the relatively restricted corpus to which these experiments have been applied so far, the technique has yielded significant results and it may become possible in the foreseeable future to apply it to more extensive bodies of semantic data.

A verifying tool more closely related to formal linguistics is the automatic comparison of machine-produced translation with a human translation of the same text. The purpose of experiments of this type is to identify problem areas in machine translation by an automatic process: the machine will print out those sentences in which a particular syntactic feature has been rendered in significantly different ways in the machine translation and in the human. The purpose of this process is to furnish the researcher with an automatically produced data file which is organized not in terms of words but in terms of pertinent syntactic problems. The computer here has taken over the initial comparison of the machine

[3] Don R. Swanson, "Searching Natural Language Text by Computer", *Science* 132:3434. 1099-1104 (Oct. 21, 1960).

output to a human product, and while the final evaluation is still the researcher's, his judgment is aided by the systematic presentation which the computer program has achieved.

4. The closest participation of the computer in the process of linguistic research takes place in the use of computing machinery to automate actual research operations. So far this computer application is only in the planning stage, but some of the plans are sufficiently detailed to deserve discussion. The use of computers to automate linguistic research procedures is based on the significance that linguists rightly attribute to the distributional description of linguistic phenomena. There are essentially two purposes to which a program based on distributional analysis can be applied: the detection of formal classes and that of semantic classes, on the basis of appropriate criteria. The former approach is the basis of my own conception of automatic linguistic analysis which I have discussed in some detail in a previous paper.[4] The latter is the basis of what has become known under the term 'distributional semantics'.

Distributional semantics is predicated on the assumption that linguistic units with certain semantic similarities also share certain similarities in the relevant environments. If therefore relevant environments can be previously specified, it may be possible to group automatically all those linguistic units which occur in similarly definable environments, and it is assumed that these automatically produced groupings will be of semantic interest. Distributional semantics is as yet a much less clearly defined area than automatic linguistic analysis.

In automatic linguistic analysis, the program contains no information about a particular language. Instead, it draws upon general assumptions about the nature of language and upon broad typological assumptions about languages of a certain structural type. Using this information, the program performs analytic operations upon a language, the specific characteristics of which are

[4] Paul L. Garvin, "Automatic linguistic analysis — a heuristic problem"' *On Linguistic Method*, pp. 78-97, The Hague, Mouton, 1964. See also pp. 23-28'

unknown to it. The program constitutes an automation of certain aspects of descriptive linguistic method; the intended output is a linguistic description. If the output is satisfactory, then the method on which the program is based can be assumed to be valid. Automatic linguistic analysis thus becomes a tool for the validation of linguistic method.

5. In summary, the criteria for our rating of these computer applications is the extent to which the computer program 'exercises' linguistic 'judgment'. In language data collection, the program is not provided with any linguistic information. It is only capable of differentiating the physical shape of input units and uses this differentiation to perform a sorting operation. In linguistic information processing and machine sentence generation, the program contains information about a particular language which permits it to differentiate certain co-occurrence properties of a language 'known' to it and to use this differentiation for a variety of purposes. In automatic linguistic analysis, the program contains information drawn from general linguistic assumptions and methods. This information enables the program to 'detect' cooccurrence properties of a language 'unknown' to it.

The 'judgment' of a computer program thus consists in the increasing diversity of conditions which it is capable of taking into account in making its string of yes/no decisions.

THE IMPACT OF LANGUAGE DATA PROCESSING ON LINGUISTIC ANALYSIS

A number of linguists have in recent years become increasingly involved in language data processing activities. The purpose of this paper is to assess the effect of this new area of interest on the field of descriptive linguistics.[1]

From a linguistic standpoint, language data processing can reasonably be defined as the application of data processing equipment to natural language text. Of greatest interest is of course the application of computing machinery.

Language data processing can either serve linguistic ends, as in automatic linguistic analysis, or more practical ends, as in the fields of machine translation, information retrieval, automatic abstracting, and related activities. The latter can be summarized under the heading of linguistic information processing.

All areas of linguistic information processing are concerned with the treatment of the content, rather than merely the form, of documents composed in a natural language. This emphasis on content constitutes one of the major differences between this aspect of language data processing and the field of descriptive linguistics as practiced in the "classical" American descriptivist tradition, where the main emphasis is on linguistic form (although even in this tradition descriptive linguists have become increasingly interested in problems of meaning).

Within the field of linguistic information processing, a major division can, from a linguist's standpoint, be made between on the one hand machine translation and on the other hand information

[1] Work on this paper was done at Thompson-Ramo-Wooldridge, Inc. under the sponsorship of the AF Office of Scientific Research of the Office of Aerospace Research, under Contract No. AF 49(638)-1128.

retrieval, automatic abstracting, and related activities. This division is based primarily on the manner in which the particular activity is concerned with the treatment of the content of the document. In machine translation, the major objective is one of recognizing the content of a document in order to render it in a different language. In the other activities, for which I have proposed the cover term content processing, recognition of the content is only the first step. More than simple rendition is required; the content of the document has to be processed further for some such purpose as the inclusion of its entirety or portions of it under index terms, or the retention of certain portions and rejection of others in order to create an extract or abstract. Content processing thus involves not only the recognition but also the evaluation of content, since for both indexing and abstracting, pertinent relevance judgments have to be applied. (See pp. 33-34).

There are two areas of language data processing in which linguistic work has found serious application in fact as well as in theory. These are automatic linguistic analysis and machine translation. While automatic linguistic analysis is as yet still in the planning stage, some of the proposed approaches are set forth in sufficient detail to deserve discussion. Machine translation has progressed beyond the planning stage some time ago, though it is still far from being fully operational. In other areas of language data processing, linguistic contributions are as yet so ill-defined that their discussion from the viewpoint of this paper is premature.

In assessing the impact of language data processing on linguistics, the empirical principle as stated by Hjelmslev[2] provides three generally acceptable evaluation criteria by its stipulation of the requirements of consistency, exhaustiveness, and simplicity. It is the contention of this paper that language data processing has served to pinpoint the difficulties that are encountered in carrying out what everybody agrees on as a desirable goal: a maximally consistent, exhaustive, and simple linguistic description.

This is most evident in the case of consistency. In data proces-

[2] See Louis Hjelmslev, *Prolegomena to a Theory of Language*, Francis Whitfield transl. (Baltimore, 1953), p. 6.

sing, inconsistency is not merely undesirable, it carries a severe penalty: it is almost trivial to make the point that a computer program just will not run unless the set of instructions is consistent within itself. The linguistic information underlying the program must obviously be equally consistent. The avoidance of inconsistency therefore becomes an overriding operational objective. The means of meeting this objective is explicitness, since this is the mechanism by which inconsistencies are uncovered for correction.

Language data processing applications require the formulation of linguistic information with a degree of explicitness that is often not met in ordinary linguistic discourse. I should like to exemplify this from the area of automatic linguistic analysis.

One of the basic assumptions of my conception of automatic linguistic analysis is that linguistic techniques can be made computable. Let me here discuss the difference in explicitness between the verbal statement of a technique and its formulation for purposes of automation.

A technique which I have found extremely useful in the syntactic analysis of an exotic language is the dropping test, serving as an operational means of ascertaining the presence of a relation of occurrence dependence (one in which a unit A presupposes a unit B for its occurrence). At the Congress in Oslo, I defined this test as follows:

> The procedure is what I have called dropping: that is, in an utterance containing both A and B (or both A, B, and C), omit one of the units and inspect the resultant truncated utterance.
>
> For occurrence dependence, the dropping test will work as follows: A is dependent on B in an utterance containing both, if an otherwise identical utterance, but from which A is dropped, is also occurrent in the text, or is accepted by the informant as viable. B is dependent on A if the utterance from which A is dropped is non-occurrent in the text, or is not accepted by the informant as viable.[3]

For the purposes of the linguistic analyst, "utterance" can be accepted as a common-sense behavioral unit, it can be assumed

[3] Paul L. Garvin, "Syntactic Units and Operations", *Proc. VIII Internat. Congress of Linguists* (Oslo, 1957), p. 629.; reprinted in *On Linguistic Method,* pp. 56-62, The Hague, Mouton & Co., 1964.

that units A and B will have been previously specified by some linguistic method, and the statements "occurrent in the text" and "accepted by the informant as viable" seem to be adequate enough descriptions of the conditions for the positive or negative result of the dropping test.

For purposes of automatic linguistic analysis (even though at present only the processing of text but not the computer simulation of informant work can be envisioned)[4] all of the above factors have to be specified in considerably more detail in order to formulate a computer subroutine simulating the dropping test:

The dropping test can be simulated by an essentially cumbersome series of comparisons (which ... can be simplified, once certain conditions are met). For each comparison, the [computer] routines will have to identify a pair of unequally long strings of elements, such that the longer of the two strings contains all the elements of the shorter one, plus one additional element. The one element present in the longer string and absent in the shorter one can be said to be 'droppable' from the longer one, if both strings have been found to recur in the text sufficiently frequently to allow the assumption that the difference in their length is not due to chance. For every identified longer string, the droppability of each element will have to be tested by finding an appropriate shorter string. Those elements for which shorter strings are not found in the input text can then be assumed not to be droppable, provided enough recurrences have been found so the that absence of a particular shorter string is not attributable to chance. In order to allow for the necessary recurrence, [an extremely] large input text would ... be required. ...

For a dropping routine to operate within the logically prescribed restrictions — that is, without an initial dictionary or grammar code — each trial would have to compare every string of n elements present in the input text to all appropriate strings of n — 1 elements. A series of passes could be envisioned, with the value of n increasing for each pass from a minimum of 2 for the first pass to the maximum found in the text, for the last pass. Assuming a punctuated text, this maximum value of n could be made very much smaller than the total number of elements in the entire text by requiring that no string be allowed to contain a

[4] This has since been envisioned in some detail. See Paul L. Garvin, "The Automation of Discovery Procedure in Linguistics", *Language 43,* 172-8 (1967); reprinted in *On Linguistic Method,* 2nd. edition, p. 38-47, The Hague, Mouton & Co., 1971.

period or other final punctuation mark — this would restrict the permissible length of a string to the span between two such punctuation marks, or between one such mark on one side, and the beginning or end of the entire text on the other. That is, the maximum permissible length of a string would be that of the longest sentence in the text.

The reverse procedure, in which the program first ascertains the maximum value for n and then decreases it with each pass, is equally thinkable.

Either procedure for applying the dropping test, to be carried to its logical conclusion, seems to require a program of quite unmanageable proportions.[5]

Let me now compare the above description of the dropping subroutine for automatic linguistic analysis to the dropping test as practiced in linguistic field work.

The first observation that can be made is that the computer simulation of the test reduces itself to a series of comparisons of strings of unequal length. Next, it may be observed that the units to be tested for droppability are in both instances either observationally given or defined by prior procedure. In the case of automatic linguistic analysis, the units dealt with are simply printed English words which by virtue of being "observable" to the input mechanism become the proper units for processing by the program. The most significant difference between the test as used in field work and its automation lies, however, in the practice of the linguistic investigator of selecting particular utterances and particular units within these utterances as the objects upon which to perform the behavioral test. In the computer subroutine as described above, this is clearly not possible, and hence its execution would result in a computer run of quite unmanageable proportions. It is, in other words, necessary to explicitate not only the conditions of the test itself, but also to explicitate the set of conditions under which the test becomes capable of execution. In my plan for auto-

[5] Paul L. Garvin, "Automatic Linguistic Analysis — A Heuristic Problem", *1961 Internat. Conf. on Machine Translation of Languages and Applied Language Analysis, National Physical Laboratory* Symposium No. 13 (London, Her Majesty's Stationery Office, 1962), p. 663; reprinted in *On Linguistic Method*, pp. 78-97, The Hague, Mouton & Co., 1964.

matic linguistic analysis, I have attempted to do this by deferring the use of dropping routines in the analysis program to a stage in the process at which the conditions for its application have been created by the use of subroutines based on other linguistic techniques. In particular, I am proposing not to use dropping routines until after the program has led to the specification of certain linguistic classes and to use the dropping routines then to test for occurrence dependences of classes of words, which can be expected to be quite finite in number, rather than for occurrence dependences of individual words, the number of which can be expected to be unmanageably large.

The essential features of the dropping test, by virtue of which it is diagnostic of a dependence relation, thus remain unaltered when the test is automated. Some important attendant conditions, on the other hand, have to be adjusted to the constraints imposed by automation: firstly, form classes which in linguistic field work are implicit in the systematic similarities of questions to informants and informant responses, must be made explicit; secondly, field work allows the random access to the ready-made store of the informant's memory, whereas in automatic linguistic analysis the necessary store of accessible forms has to be prepared by previous procedures.

Let me now turn to the questions of exhaustiveness and simplicity. I should like to discuss these on the basis of some illustrations taken from machine translation.

First, the matter of exhaustiveness. This is one of the most difficult requirements to define in linguistic analysis. I have commented on it in a previous context, and at that time I stated that a significant consideration is whether or not the analyst is dealing with classes of unrestricted or restricted membership.[6] In the first case, exhaustiveness can only be achieved by a listing of classes, since obviously a complete listing of an unlimited membership is self-contradictory. In the second case, a listing of not only all

[6] Paul L. Garvin, "On the Relative Tractability of Morphological Data", *Word* 13, 22-3 (1957); reprinted in On Linguistic Method, pp. 22-35, The Hague, Mouton & Co., 1964.

classes but also of all members is possible. This is, however, a purely theoretical definition of exhaustiveness. It does not touch upon the heart of the matter, which is the extent to which exhaustiveness can be achieved, or must be achieved, in a particular task of linguistic analysis and how the requirement can be met in practice. In machine translation, the program as was stated further above is to a significant extent based upon a linguistic description of the source language. Since the aim of machine translation research is to produce ultimately a program that will be capable of dealing with randomly selected text, the question of exhaustiveness is of extreme practical importance and has to be faced from the beginning. There are two areas in which the problem of exhaustiveness arises: first, the lexicon, where in machine translation the problem concerns the machine dictionary; second, the grammatical description of the language, where in machine translation the grammar code and the syntax routines of the translation algorithm are involved. The field has not yet progressed sufficiently to allow the inclusion of problems of semantic equivalence and multiple-meaning resolution in the present discussion.[7]

Operationally, the problem is that the research has to be conducted, and the system developed, in stages. This remains equally true if the point of view is adopted that a complete linguistic description must precede the development of a machine translation system; such a prior complete description must still be prepared gradually. In either case, research in stages means dealing with one linguistic problem area at a time, without violating the requirement of exhaustiveness. The planning of the research stages thus becomes the primary question.

The details of planning for exhaustiveness involve the following:

In machine translation research, it is not possible to use the convenient scholarly device of the "et cetera", or of suggesting,

[7] Don R. Swanson, "The Nature of Multiple Meaning", *Proceedings of the National Symposium on Machine Translation.* H. P. Edmundson, ed. (Englewood Cliffs, N. J., 1961), p. 386: "Now that the stage has been set in previous discussion by the picturing of polysemia as a 'monster' or a 'blank wall', let me say that there isn't a great deal more to be said about multiple meaning that isn't either obvious or else wrong. ..."

"If this technique is carried further, it will then allow the treatment of the rest of the data".[8] The computer will not accept this kind of instruction. It is therefore necessary to make other provisions for exhaustiveness in spite of the limited scope of the dictionary and syntax program that the realities permit at any one given stage before the final aim has been achieved.

In regard to the machine dictionary, the question of exhaustiveness as to the number of dictionary entries is not of great theoretical interest, since it differs very little from the problem of exhaustiveness faced by lexicography in general. The only problem faced by machine translation researchers is that of having efficient procedures for dictionary updating, and this problem has been solved satisfactorily by most groups.

The question of making provisions for exhaustiveness in the actual translation algorithm is much more interesting. It must first be noted that there are essentially two technical aspects to every computer program: first, a table-lookup procedure, in which the program looks up information in a table for use in later processing; second, a logical-tree-type algorithm, in which the program goes through a series of yes-no decisions (often based on information looked up in a table), in order to arrive at an appropriate end result. Provisions for exhaustiveness here consist essentially in writing a program that allows room for later additions as more information becomes known and can be included. The "et cetera" is replaced by a more explicit device. In the tables of a program, provisions for the addition of further information are made by leaving sufficient blank fields, that is, spaces to be taken up by later instructions and information. An important consideration in the design of the program then becomes the size of these fields that are to be left blank for later use. In a logical-tree-type algorithm, provisions for later additions can be made by building into the

[8] Cf. George L. Trager and Henry Lee Smith, Jr., *Outline of English Structure* (= *Studies in Linguistics, Occasional Papers* No. 3) (Norman, Okla., 1951), p. 55: "A full presentation would [include a complete description of phonemics, morphophonemics, morphology, and syntax] ... No such full grammar is attempted here. The purpose is to present enough material for discussion to illustrate the procedures and techniques involved".

algorithm end points to which further branches can be added by which to treat information that may later turn out to be of importance. Thus, the linguist's statement that "additional data can be handled by the same technique" is replaced by an open-ended exit in the program.

In the Fulcrum I machine translation program (see pp. 83-89), this can be exemplified by the blank fields that are contained in the grammar code for the addition of grammatical information for which plans were laid down, but which it was not yet possible to pin down sufficiently to include in the program. The open-ended exits are exemplified by the provisions of the syntax program to print out under certain conditions "notices of syntactic difficulty" whenever the algorithm for coping with such a difficulty has not yet been written.

Now to consider the matter of simplicity. I have on a previous occasion pointed out the difficulty inherent in a criterion of simplicity.[9] At that time I raised the question of defining simplicity more clearly by stipulating whether or not it is to be gauged in terms of minimizing the inventory of units, or by minimizing the number of rules. It seems to me now that the question cannot be answered in the abstract. It is impossible to specify the simplicity of a sequence of procedural steps or of the logical structure of a description in an objective way. It is too much a matter of esthetics.

It is not unreasonable, on the other hand, to attempt to specify simplicity in terms of the attainment of a particular aim, such as efficiency in the use of equipment. I should like to exemplify this by a brief discussion of the grammar code used in the Fulcrum I machine translation program.

The purpose of this grammar code is to provide all the grammatical information that is required for the efficient operation of the syntax routines. One important task of these routines is to carry out an agreement check, that is, to ascertain on the basis of the grammar codes that have been furnished to the program whether or not certain adjacent words are in grammatical agree-

[9] Paul L. Garvin, review of *Prolegomena to a Theory of Language* by Louis Hjelmslev, in *Language* 30 (1954), 70.

ment with each other, such as for instance a noun and preceding adjectives. For purposes of maximum efficiency of operation, a grammar code was devised which takes up more space in the computer memory but allows the rapid completion of agreement checks by a computer operation similar to ordinary subtraction of one digit at a time, an operation called "masking". The drawback of this type of grammar code is that it takes up a considerable amount of memory space. From the standpoint of storage, a grammar code compressed into the minimum amount of space is obviously vastly preferable.

It turns out, therefore, that in this particular case the requirement of simplicity has to be formulated quite differently in terms of the different purposes to which a particular set of elements is put. For purposes of the operation of agreement checks, a grammar code spread out over more space but allowing rapid completion of the check, is the most efficient and consequently the simplest. For purposes of saving memory space, the maximally condensed code is most efficient. It is thus possible to formulate a requirement of simplicity — if one equates efficiency with simplicity — quite clearly in terms of a particular purpose.[10]

The above discussion may explain why I have come to regard language data processing a very important application of linguistics. It is a challenge to linguistics as a science. The challenge is not theoretical, but operational — it is directed at both the methods and the results of linguistics. The strong requirement of exhaustiveness forces the treatment of minor subpatterns of a language, and not merely of its major patterns.

By enforcing its requirements, the computer has become an analytical instrument for linguistics, where previously only recording instruments were available. This may have important theoretical implications.

[10] Both solutions were used in the Fulcrum I machine translation program. The grammar code was stored in its condensed form, and a simple subroutine was applied to transform the condensed grammar code into the spread-out grammar code for use in agreement checking.

SUBJECT INDEX

Note: The abbreviation ff. following a page number refers to all following pages until the end of that chapter.

NAME INDEX

Bei Fragen zur Produktsicherheit wenden Sie sich bitte an:
If you have any questions regarding product safety,
please contact:

Walter de Gruyter GmbH
Genthiner Straße 13
10785 Berlin
productsafety@degruyterbrill.com